Unlocking the Small Business Game

The Playbook for Starting a Small Business from Nothing Using Simple Clear Uncommon Sense

By W. James Dennis

Sign-up now for free news, reports, discounts and advanced access to future books and courses. All for free. To learn more visit:

www.wjamesd.com/free-stuff

Unlocking the Small Business Game
The Playbook for Starting a Small Business from Nothing Using Simple Clear Uncommon Sense

Limits of Liability/Disclaimer of Warranty
The author of this book has used his best effort in preparing this material. The author makes no representation or warranties with respect to the accuracy, applicability, suitability or completeness of this book's contents. The author disclaims any warranties (expressed or implied), merchantability or suitability for any particular purpose. The author shall in no event be held liable for any loss or other damages, including but not limited to special, incidental, consequential or other damages. As always, the advice of a competent legal, tax, accounting or other professional should be sought.

First Edition (*rm*)

ISBN – 978-0-9915587-0-4 (ebk)
ISBN – 978-0-9915587-1-1 (sc)

Cover Design and Image Consultation by Bryan R. Lewis

Contents

Forward
THE OUTLOOK

"Things may come to those who wait, but only the things left by those who hustle."
- Abraham Lincoln

First and foremost thank you for your purchase. Rest assured, I think our journey will be an eye-opener.

First let's get some minor things out of the way shall we?

I am in no way offering you legal advice. I recommend that you seek out books or go online to acquire information that will help you set-up a business legally in your state and county. This book is about making money and keeping it – Hustling.

Next up is how I'm going to present this material to you. I am going to be talking to you in plain English. No fluff and unnecessary concepts. I will (as much as possible) write how I speak so I may use terms that are unfamiliar to you. I will do my best to define these terms. If I didn't learn anything else, I learned that keeping things simple is the strongest way to communicate. I wish I had a book like this when I first set foot into the world of business. My goal was to make this book just that. One last thing.

This book has been written to offer the perspective of someone who has very little money but has a desire to be an entrepreneur. This makes you a Hustler. I will define the term for you in a moment. I need you to know that everything you will read in this book can be applied to 90% of businesses out there. But even then, you will find some useful points in this book that may change your perspective on how to approach situations in your market or industry.

So What Is A Hustler?

A modern day Hustler is not what you're seeing in the movies or on television. When most people read or hear the word Hustler their imagination immediately goes into thinking about some con-artist, a trickster or someone who basically deceives people for money. Another immediate thought is a drug-dealer. Well, to really get a proper definition, why don't you ask someone who carries the title? Would you ask someone who spent their life as a pastry Chef about fixing cars? No you wouldn't. So it takes a Hustler to define just exactly what a Hustler is.

The word Hustler means entrepreneur. That's all! Over the decades it has become a street term to define someone who makes money anyway they can by using all the resources available to them.

A Hustler doesn't wait for an opportunity when they can create their own. They make sense out of what appears to the average person to be non-sense. They use their talents and abilities wisely to secure advantages for themselves and this reflects in their entrepreneurial endeavors.

A Hustler has to be able to maneuver through dark corridors with no flashlight. They have to have a natural sense of direction and be self-reliant.

To put it plainly, if you're a car salesperson, you're a Hustler. If you own a small business, you're a Hustler. If you're involved in a Network Marketing company, you're a Hustler.

The biggest Hustlers are those that sit and run large corporations. They make a lot of money, they do it every day and they do it using all the resources and advantages they have available to them. That's real hustling! The fact of the matter is – you deal with Hustlers almost every day of your life.

Now the "street" Hustler begins his or her enterprise on the streets. They are a mobile business. Some businesses thrive like this, for others this is just a stepping stone to greater heights.

Allow me to illustrate this – Let's say you bake cookies. You've been doing it for years and you love making them. You know in your heart that your cookies are better than anything you've ever tasted before. Even your friends beg you for them all the time and they all agree – they're damn good.

You decide to begin making batches of them at night. Then you package them up in little bags. Say, five cookies per bag. What are you going to do with these little bags? Well you're going to take them to your job and sell them. You will give out free samples, sell your cookie bags for a reasonable price and even begin to take orders.

As the word spreads you begin to make more variety of cookies, take more orders and of course make more money.

Then what? Well then you begin to work through other people. You let them take your cookies to other places, maybe their place of worship, maybe to their book club meetings. They have no problem doing that. They want to help you and you give them something in return for their efforts. And over time your business takes off! If you don't think something like this is possible I just have two words for you.

Famous Amos.

Ever had a Famous Amos cookie? Chances are you've had at least one. And even if you haven't, you more than likely know the name.

If you're willing to learn and use the tools I have for you here, you can take almost anything and create a whole business around it. Now, some things sell much better than others but we'll talk about that in time. I just wanted you to see the potential of what we Hustlers call the "Grind". It's the work we put into our enterprises to make them successful. But this work must be done properly for the fastest and best results, are you with me so far?

A Hustler has a unique perspective on business and life in general. While you look at things, a Hustler sees through them. Hustling is a set of skills and you will learn many of them as they apply to small business in this book.

"A solid goal with a unique effort put in will always pay off."
- W. James Dennis

A Little About Me

I've always wanted to be an entrepreneur; ever since I was 15 years old in fact. I used to watch my father time and again start businesses and this intrigued me. Now, my father never actually followed through with his businesses but watching him rubbed off on me.

When I was 15, I got my first job. It was after school for about three hours a day. I used to clean up a middle school that was near my house. I was a janitor. I cleaned class rooms, emptied trashcans, washed chalkboards and scrapped gum off of the floor, you get my point.

Now it was only three hours a day, Monday through Friday, but I could already see how putting in work like this for 40 hours a week was not going to be what I wanted in life. Many of you feel the same way, I'm sure.

I began to try to get my hands on business books. I was 15, what did I know about business? My father and I weren't close so it was difficult to go to him on the subject. And plus I always liked to find things out on my own anyway. I was very hard-headed then and still can be; most entrepreneurs are to some degree.

I studied book after book. Then I began to buy courses through the mail. Some of the information was good. Most of it was just plain garbage. "Fools writing books for profit," as I like to call them. Over the next three or four years I grew increasingly frustrated with all this useless information so I turned my mind towards other things. Now at 20, those other things were mostly young ladies, but the workings of the mind fascinated me as well. But that inner entrepreneurial spark never left. It would take some years to turn that spark into a fire.

That spark was ignited by a Hustler. This man taught me more about business than I had learned in 20 books. And once I got the courage to go out and do it for myself I ran into more Hustlers that would complete my business "education". They made concepts so simple and best of all I could see how they worked in real time. If they lied, it would show immediately because it wouldn't yield results.

Because of this I began to realize that maybe I was learning things backwards in the past. I was learning about how to run a huge enterprise, but I didn't have big money or a big budget. I also didn't have the credit to get a loan. But I didn't need one after all. All I needed was the right kind of information and the understanding of how to use it. And now I present this information to you.

Like a nurse has to learn medical terminology and the workings of the body before they practice on patients, you have to first learn the "Game" before you practice business concepts. So I will now introduce you to them. If being a Hustler is **in** you, you will know it after reading just the first three chapters. The workings of the "Game" are just that powerful.

Take what you need from this book and develop from there. To your success!

CHAPTER 1

"The Game" – So, What Are We Playing?

There is a "Game" to business, and that game is survival. Most people tell you the purpose of business is to make a profit and that is true, that is its **purpose**, but that is not the Game we're playing.

Just as a human being needs food, water and air to survive at the most basic level a business needs cash flow to keep it alive.

A business can fail to make a profit for a quarter or two, or even a few years, but if that business can survive, it has the potential to eventually turn a profit. If the business cannot survive, then there is absolutely no potential for profit. And if there is no profit, there will be no growth. And anything that does not change and grow will eventually die.

As a human being you can live a few days without food and water as long as you have air; a business can survive for a time without cash flow as long as there is still something it can sell. Both the human and business may eventually die by "just barely holding on," but there is a chance that fighting just one more day may turn things around for the better.

So the Game we're playing as enterprising Hustlers is survival. For those of you who want a technical term for this, it is called "Creating a sustainable business model". I'm going to teach you how to establish this for yourself.

The most important thing that you must come to terms with is that you must change your paradigm. You can't be your own boss, if you're still thinking like a common employee. Being a boss is great. You have a certain degree of freedom but you also take on all the risk. Have you ever sat on your job and thought that it's not fair that the owner of your company makes his fortune off of your hard work? Then I have to tell you, you're looking at the Game wrong.

Let me change your paradigm (thought pattern). Is it fair that your boss makes money off of all your blood, sweat and tears? Yes it is. As an employee you can go search for employment elsewhere, the owner however is trapped. He or she can't really jump ship; if the ship goes down, they have to sink with it. More freedom, more responsibility but more risk.

There is one major rule in this Game and that rule is: You must give in order to receive; everything in business has its price. You have to pay to play.

Here's a truth that you may not want to hear, but it's part of the Game of business and needs to be said. Not too far in the past, wealth was built not on people **winning**, but by people **losing**. Some forms of business still run by this model. Just think of the lottery for example, casinos and the tobacco industry.

In the United States back in the mid 1800's there was a phenomena called the "Gold Rush". Tens of thousands of people from the Eastern and Northern parts of America as well as from other countries all heeded the call of, "Go West young man, go West!"

There was gold to be found in California and the Rocky Mountains and people uprooted their families and headed West all with a dream of striking it rich.

The majority of people did not strike it rich. A small number found gold but not enough to maintain a stable lifestyle.

Now here's some business Game for you. The majority of the miners did not get rich. Do you know who did get rich during the Gold Rush? The supply merchants. The people who profited the most from other people's dreams (the miners) were the merchants who sold the equipment and provisions necessary to mine gold. Think about it. You can't mine gold without equipment, everyone mining needs it. Now that's Hustling.

Times have changed however; the old business model has to be reversed in order to survive in today's economy. The consumer has to win, and the business has to win. If the customer feels as though he or she hasn't won then say goodbye to your business cash flow and prepare to bury the dead.

The first step in unlocking the small business Game is realizing that you are in a "Game" to begin with. Every Game has a structure and rules and if you know these rules and know how to play, you can excel in it with enough practice.

Take a look at these facts. At the time of this writing, 25% of businesses fail within their first year. I'm very familiar with this; my first two businesses failed in their first year.

Another 23% of businesses will fail before they hit the four year mark. On average only 44% of businesses make it past the fifth year. What happens, why do over half of businesses fail?

The number one reason is incompetence. Poor pricing practices, lack of record keeping and/or finances and non-payment of taxes.

The number two reason is lack of managerial experience. Not budgeting correctly, expanding too fast and borrowing too much.

Do you see a pattern here? The problem is cash flow; either the lack of it or the mismanagement of it.

This is the Game ladies and gentlemen. A business must survive. Your entire business needs to be based around this fact. Anything that threatens your business's survival needs to be taken care of with no hesitation. Or better yet, structure your business so that you can avoid a lot of these pitfalls altogether.

If you are in the Game, you are a player. But no matter how hard or how well you play, the Game cannot exist without the customer. Let's be clear on this rule, there is no Game without someone wanting to purchase something.

As we continue our journey we will explore concepts that will help you make your way through dark corridors without a flashlight. But first we need to change another one or your paradigms. Let's talk about the work ethic of the self-employed, the independent Hustler.

CHAPTER 2
"The Grind" – Why Hustlers Hustle

Let's get straight into it! I want to introduce you to a character I'll make reference to from time to time while reading this entire book. We'll call him Michael. Michael is a tried and true Hustler. He is an independent business owner and entrepreneur who has put in time and effort to create a successful company for himself.

What does Michael do? He sells sport T-shirts (Tee's) and sports caps. Good quality stuff, at a fair price. He does more than that but let's just keep it simple for now. Say hello and good-bye to Michael the Hustler for a moment.

So what exactly is "The Grind", you ask? Well allow me to elaborate a little. A Hustler (entrepreneur) is tied to three main things:

(1) The Goal – This can be anything that the Hustler is trying to accomplish. It of course usually requires money and the freedom to enjoy it.

(2) The Game – We gave an overview of this in Chapter One. There is more to it of course, but for now realize that if you don't play the Game, the Game will play you so to speak. When it is all said and done, there is only one Game. There are many markets and industries, but every market and industry is still dependant on the Game itself.

(3) The Grind – "The Grind" is the actual work that goes into The Game to get out of it what you want. What you're trying to get out of The Game is the accomplishment of your goals. It's as simple as that.

This is a Hustler's personal trinity. We learn **Game** and **Grind** to get what we **need** and **want**. Simple.

So when you hear a Hustler talk about they are on their Grind, you know that they are working to achieve their goal. "Work now, rest when you're dead," or "Stay hungry." Both these sayings draw the same conclusion.

One reason why the word Grind is used instead of the word "work" is really a mental thing. Work brings the image into most people's mind as a 9-to-5 job. Hustlers don't work for someone else, they Grind for themselves. Since you now are familiar with the term Grind, I'll be using this term and the word "work" interchangeably.

In a 9-to-5 job you do your eight hours then go home. And if you're not a manager or an owner that's all you *want* to do. Not for a Hustler (entrepreneur). A Hustler doesn't work, we grind. We make it a point to put in as much time, sweat and energy as necessary every day we go out to do business.

If that means four hours, we're ok with that. If that means 10 hours, no problem. If it means we have to work in the dead of night at three in the morning sitting in our office, then that's where we'll be. There are no hourly restrictions when it comes to the almighty Grind. The Game itself doesn't stop, the best you can do is to just play as hard as you can. Make no mistake though; we do strive to maintain a balance in our lives. All work and no play will lead to burn out. And you're no good to anyone when you're burnt out.

Alright moving on… let's say you work a standard 9-to-5 job like any good employee. You work eight hours a day and five days a week. Meaning, you get paid for working 40 hours a week.

To keep things as simple as possible, let's just say you make ten dollars an hour at this job. Small change I know but stay with me here. And get out a calculator if you're slow in math like I am. I'll be going fast here and I don't want to lose you.

At this ten dollar an hour job you "gross" (money before taxes are taken out) sixteen-hundred dollars ($1,600).

$10 an hour times eight hours a day = $80
$80 a day times five days a week = $400
$400 a week times four weeks in a month = $1,600

Now remember, this is all before you pay your taxes! So let's take out a measly hundred dollars for taxes. I know this is a very unrealistic figure but I want to keep this simple so you can see the power of the grind.

So after taxes you are left with fifteen-hundred dollars ($1,500) a month. That is your "net", meaning cash in your pocket. Alright now let's look at Michael the Hustler's numbers shall we (remember him)?

Michael sells his basic Tee's for ten dollars each. If Michael sold one Tee every hour for eight hours he will bring in the same amount of money as your nine to five job.

One Tee sold at $10, every hour for 8 hours a day = $80

If he did this five days a week for the whole month he would have made sixteen-hundred dollars ($1,600) for that month. Are you still with me?

Let's stop here a moment. In business, it usually takes money to make money. Michael had to buy those shirts before he could resale them. Let's say Michael buys his Tee's wholesale for five dollars and resells them for ten dollars. So he is only actually "netting" (cash in his pocket) five dollars for every shirt he sells. He only keeps half of the ten dollars as profit (five dollars).

Again, Michael sales for ten dollars but he spent five dollars for the **opportunity** to bring in ten dollars. So he only profits five dollars.

This means that at the end of the month his "gross" is sixteen-hundred dollars ($1,600) but since he has to pay for his products he only will see half of that in his pocket, his "net" (profit) is only eight hundred dollars ($800). If I lost you then please go back and re-read it. This is very important.

Now in order for Michael to pocket the same amount of money you do in your nine to five job, he must sell at least two Tee's an hour, not one. Those two Tee's will bring him in twenty dollars an hour. Ten dollars of that money will go back to buying more Tee's from the wholesaler. This means Michael is left with ten dollars cash in his pocket (profit).

2 Tee's sold at $10 for that hour = $20
2 Tee's bought at $5 each from the wholesaler = $10
$20 from the 2 Tee's that sold minus $10 for what Michael paid for them = $10 in profit
$10 in profit per hour for 8 hours = $80 (the same as a $10 an hour job)

Now before you feel bad for Michael cause he has to sell two Tee's every hour to make what you make at your 9-to-5 job, I want you to remember that our man Michael is a true Hustler. He doesn't sell two Tee's an hour. He sells more like six! So in effect he "grosses" sixty dollars an hour. He profits half of that to bring his "net" income to thirty dollars an hour! How much is that a month? For a month that is, Four-thousand and eight hundred dollars ($4,800). That's money in his pocket, spendable cash. Of course he needs to pay taxes and other fees, but that's a pretty comfortable living for a single man with no children, wouldn't you agree?

Now what if Michael stepped up his Game (business) to sell just seven shirts an hour? How about 10? If he sold 10 shirts an hour his monthly, cash in pocket income, would be eight-thousand dollars ($8,000). That's ninety-six thousand ($96,000) a year "net" compared to your eighteen-thousand ($18,000) a year job (after taxes)! Do the math for yourself.

Is this realistic? Not entirely, it's a very simplistic model but I hope you see my point. The best part is Michael did this with complete control of his time. He didn't sell 10 shirts an hour completely on his own (that's like owning a job – not what we're trying to do in the long run), but you can't deny that this math is extremely motivating.

This is why a Hustler hustles; to take charge of their financial life and to be their own boss. They desire to live life on their own terms. Although the word Grind can be defined as hard work, the Grind we're talking about in this book is much more than that. We are building a business also. We have to look ahead and strategize and play the Game correctly, this process is also part of the Grind.

CHAPTER 3
"The Chain" – How Money Flows

I know you're probably ready to get started into some of the techniques and other things, but there is one more principle you need to understand before we continue.

This principle is the muscle that will surround the bones of your business Game. If you completely understand what I have to tell you here, you will further understand why some people never succeed in business.

Remember, survival is the Game we are playing. People blame the economy, horrible timing or bad partners for their failure and more than 50% of the time that is not the case. These people started their venture with the wrong mindset and the wrong information. They were destined to fail. If you constantly look up while you walk, you will miss the downward staircase in front of you. Ouch!

Did you know that almost 95% of the people in the United States will die broke? Why is that? Well a large reason is because we're never taught about money. We are taught how to make it for someone else (work), we are taught how to spend it, save it and more importantly we're taught the only value it has is to get things we want. All this is backwards!

Do me a favor real fast. Take a single dollar bill out of your pocket for me. Some of you still do carry cash don't you? If you don't have one then grab a quarter, any coin, I don't care. Now what do you see when you look at money? A way to pay bills? Buy that new house or car? A way to buy food and other basic necessities of life?

Let me tell you what a Hustler sees when they look at a dollar. They see a hand full of dollars. They understand that money should be used to make more money first. Everything else comes after that. A Hustler is willing to sacrifice comfort now, for greater comfort later. And later is the time when they have the extra money to do so.

The Philosophy of "The Flip"

I will get into more depth about this later but for now understand this. That dollar you see must be made to make more of itself. That dollar should not "die" before it "multiplies". That one dollar must be made into three dollars. One of those three dollars is used to re-invest in your business to keep it running. The second dollar is put aside to grow your business (investing for the future). And that third dollar is what you live off of. Think about that for a moment.

Every time you spend a dollar without "flipping" it first (making that dollar grow into more), you are literally cutting your own throat financially. Period, end of story.

You must learn, like I did, that it's not about saving money. It's about having your money make you money. Once you get on that level, you are on the road to financial freedom.

Do not misread me here. Yes, you need to enjoy yourself! You need to treat yourself, your family and loved ones, just realize that for the long-term, you must learn to flip money. And eventually have it flip itself; have your money make money.

"Scared money doesn't make money." This old Hustler saying means that you must be willing to invest in yourself. You must be willing to spend the money properly in order for it to grow. If not, then I'll have to give you another quote, "A fool and his money soon part."

Don't be that fool any longer!

You pay your household bills, don't you? And you pay for car insurance, gas, clothes, food, cell phone bill and possibly day care. You get your paycheck on your job and you pay all of these companies, but you don't pay yourself first. You worked for it, pay yourself first!

A Hustler is about flipping money before it's spent. And you need to understand why. Let's look at a standard business model here in the United States and most parts of the World.

The Infamous Money Chain

You go to your local store and purchase a microwave. It's new, it's shiny and you feel you need it so you buy it. Now, where is this money going? It's goes up the chain so to speak. That microwave you just bought allows the retail store you just purchased it from to buy another microwave and make a profit.

But where do they get the microwave from? The microwave comes from a wholesaler. And where does the wholesaler get it from? Most times it comes from a distributor. And the distributor gets it from the manufacturer (the actual maker of the product).

The money you just spent on the microwave goes all the way up the chain (the money flows up). I'll illustrate this for you so you can get a visual.

Manufacture
Distributor
Wholesaler
Retailer
Consumer

Now everyone in this chain gets money except for whom? That's right, the consumer. They don't get any money. They are giving their money to those above the chain. All the consumer gets is the end product. This is a fair exchange.

Now sometimes there is no distributor, and sometimes the wholesaler can be cut out of a deal, but the model for the most part gives us something to work with. If you always stay a consumer, you will never make money! So step one is to get yourself up a level on the chain to becoming a retailer. So, how do you do that?

Simply find something that can be sold.

Let's revisit Michael the Hustler. He sells Tee's and sports caps. He purchases these from a wholesaler (or distributor) and sells them at a retail price to the consumer. He is essentially a retailer.

Does he get a lot of money? He gets enough; but not as much as he could be getting.

If our Hustler Michael were to stack (save) and then invest his money, he would be able to buy large quantities directly from the distributor or manufacturer and his price per each piece would go down. He could skip the wholesaler.

In our previous example he paid five dollars each for his Tee's. If he could buy thousands at a time he could probably get them for maybe two dollars each. I'm just keeping this simple here.

Now would Michael still be a retailer at this level? Possibly, if he was sure he could sell thousands of Tee's a month. But since he is now getting his Tee's for only two dollars, he could find other retailers to sell to; he could move a hell of a lot more Tee's this way than he could move by himself as only a retailer. He would charge these retailers five dollars per shirt. He would at this point become a wholesaler. He just moved another link up the chain.

The higher you go up the chain, the more money there is. Stop and think about this a minute. Think about how it can be applied to your business or the business you plan on starting.

Now here's a twist for you. Michael can get paid in two ways now. He has more advantages at this point. He can wholesale his products and still sell them retail. He just created two income streams; wholesale and retail. And since he only pays two dollars each for the Tee's now, he is making more money in the retail end by still selling at ten dollars.

If Michael the Hustler continued to work his way up the chain to the manufacturer level, he would be an extremely wealthy individual, don't you agree?

He could sell retail on his own, sell to other retailers, sell to wholesalers, and sell to distributors. Although at this point, selling retail is a waste of time (and illegal if done improperly).

Do you think Wal-Mart has gotten as big as it has by just selling on the retail level? Wal-Mart distributes their own brands of food, clothing and housewares. Then they sell them directly out of their own stores. They make money retailing other company's goods and they also distribute (and sometimes manufacture) their own goods, skipping wholesale completely. That's Hustling.

This, my friend, is the Infamous Money Chain and this is why a True Hustler does not waste those precious dollars. This is why a True Hustler stays on their Grind (works hard to make their business grow). They strive to move up the chain, and you can't do that if you're broke.

Fantastic! Now that you understand what we're working with here, let's get on to more important things. Like, how exactly can you start with almost nothing and create a profitable small or home-based business?

I'm glad you asked; let's dig right in shall we?

CHAPTER 4

First Key; First Lock

Business is simple. It is not always easy; it may be the hardest work you will ever do in your life – but the core of business is not complicated.

Now you have to understand the following principle, it will simplify every single business decision you make from this point on. Again, I don't care if you haven't started yet, or have been in business for years. I don't care if you're in a Network Marketing company. This business Game knowledge is universal. It works every single time and in any economy.

Let's stop here for a moment. Let's say that the American economy went through another depression like it did in the 1930's. What is the one single most important thing that every person and business would want? Easy question to answer, they want to survive and that means they want to make more money. If you could show people how to do that, don't you think you would be a very wealthy person? Let's get into this a little further.

Before I get you too excited, I need to let you know that this key only unlocks the first lock of small business Game. This is a small piece of a bigger picture.

Ready to change your mind about business forever?

Let me tell you a short story, it will illustrate what I'm trying to say. One of my first businesses was selling silver jewelry. Now, I had taken most of my last two paychecks to get this started. I had two close friends of mine who invested also. We operated separately, but under the same business license. The money they made was theirs, and the money I made was mine. We did agree though to put money into a pot to grow the business and we also would split the tax costs when that time rolled around.

I had no clue what I was doing! I read the books, yes. I studied, I tried to stay positive but I could not figure out quite how to do the most important thing in business. Get customers! Customers create cash flow after all.

We resorted to trying things out on the streets. We didn't have a store and we only had two cars between the three of us (mine had recently been repossessed, go figure). We made nice cases to keep the jewelry in so it could be displayed and we set out to make money. I guess you can see what happened at this point.

Day after day we went out, over and over. I for one didn't make enough money to cover my bills. And I didn't have a paycheck coming in either! I failed, and failed miserably. But I did take the risk, I just took it blindly. This little stunt landed me having to live with my ex-girlfriend. I was broke and had no place else to live.

It was almost two years later, during my next job, that I encountered a true Hustler that began to teach me the ropes. He was even kind enough to show me where he was getting a few of his products wholesale.

Once I got the hang of things, I threw caution to the wind and took one-hundred and fifty dollars out of my last paycheck and ventured off again. I had many setbacks, but I finally succeeded. What changed? My outlook on business and the Game I was playing. What this Hustler told me was, "Your job is to just get the people what they want. That's it."

Ok, ok it was a little more than that but if I had to translate everything he said into one sentence, it would be the following:

You are in business to solve people's problems!

People spend money to solve their problems. There is a deeper level to that which I'll explain in much detail later, but for now let me explain this. When you are hungry you have a problem, right? What do you do? You go get food whether it's at a grocery store or from a fast food restaurant or something classier. You eat, problem solved.

Your car needs tires. Now that's a problem, right? What do you do? You go to a place that sells tires and purchase some new ones. Simple. You find out that your roof is leaking. What do you do? Well if you're renting you call the landlord. But even if you own your home, the end result is that a roofer is called in to fix it.

You must find a problem and a way to solve it. When you do, people will pay you for it. People want results! And they want them as fast as possible. To make a quote, "If you build a better mouse trap, the World with beat a path to your door." and I would have to add, "Especially if mice were a huge problem."

My silver jewelry business failed because I did not find the people with the problem! I did not seek out the people who buy silver, love to buy it and felt that they needed it. If I would have found these people, been able to offer great quality and a damn good deal, I would have made it!

And let me take this up another level. If I was really smart, I wouldn't have been selling silver jewelry in the first place. I would have found a more pressing problem that people would be even more willing to pay for. Silver would have been good money, but slow money. Hustlers don't like slow money unless it's a long-term investment. With that being said, the internet was still in its infancy back then. The internet as it is today could have substantially changed my business. Back to the point.

To make money, you need to identify a problem for people, and have a way to solve it. Better yet, don't concentrate so much on **selling** a product or service. Concentrate on solving people's problem **with** your product or service.

This ever so small change of focus is one big difference between succeeding in business and failing. And if you're in a Network Marketing company (or professional sales), this is the key to building rapport with a potential prospect. Put the selling down for a moment (don't drop it, just put it on the shelf for awhile) and concentrate on helping them with their problem.

What exactly is a problem? Simply put, it's anything that the person cannot solve without help. Whether they sincerely need the help or just do not have the time to solve the problem for themselves.

The key is: If the problem is big enough to them, they will be willing to pay more for a solution. Let me say that again. The bigger the person **perceives** the problem to be, the more they will pay for a fast solution.

Now in order for you to help them, you must first identify their problem. And how can you do that? It's just a matter of asking. That's it! If you learn to keep things simple, you will be that much closer to being successful.

Let me break this down for you even further. If you can solve their problem, quickly, honestly, with good quality (it doesn't always have to be the best) and at a reasonable price then guess what? You have just created a loyal customer. This is one of the keys to getting customers (we'll talk about keeping them a little later), and getting customers is the most important thing for a business.

Nothing happens until something is sold. If you don't sell anything, then nothing will happen. Learn to help first. If your product or service can be the solution to the problem, it will sell itself. All you have to do is present it to them and explain how it will help. That's your job, plain and simple.

Stop letting people tell you that you must sell, sell, sell! That if you don't sell then you will fail and your business will not last. You want the truth? Can you handle it? Can you let go of all the misconceptions you've been fed about business?

Here is the truth. No one, I repeat, no one likes to be sold something! You know this is true because you, yourself, don't like to be sold something. But everyone likes for their problems to be solved. This, my friend, is called "building value" also called a "value proposition" for my technical readers.

If the **perceived** value of your product or service is high, you will make money. In fact, there's no way you can't! Find a problem, find a solution, get the solution to the people and make money. Got that? Great!

We've covered the Hustler's personal trinity, now I will lay out the business trinity.

(1) Perception – Perception is King. The way something is perceived is what gives it value. One man's junk is another man's treasure; better said, nothing has value until someone gives it value. You and your company must be unique and if you can add in a unique product or service, you are well on your way. Control the perception of your business and brand. We will speak more about perception later on.

(2) Delivery – You must deliver! Your business must deliver – at all times, no exceptions. You cannot satisfy everyone, but that should never stop you or slow you down from delivering 100% to each and every person you do business with.

(3) Repetition – You have to lead. I'm not talking about being first in your particular market because you don't have to in order to have a successful small business. But you have to lead your customers, those adoring fans or yours. You must lead them to buy from you, repeatedly, by offering something new and greater. Or, depending on your business, doing what you do so well and consistently that they don't want to go anywhere else. Some Hustlers call this "funneling". Just like an actual funnel, the customer spins around and around multiple times in your funnel before they come out of the bottom end.

Now, to do this the right way you need the right tools. And I will give them to you now. In our next three chapters I will give you the three most important tools a Hustler needs for success. These tools represent a foundation. Think of them as the roots of a tree. If the tree's roots are deep and strong, the tree will be around for centuries. No wind or storm can come and just knock it over. It may lose some leaves and branches, but the trunk of that tree isn't going anywhere. So what are these three tools?

#1 – The Mind: The proper mindset and way of thinking about business. Without the proper mindset, nothing else you do will be effective. In fact without this mindset, you will cut your chances of success by 50%. This is the most important tool.

#2 – The Body: How to move and dress for success. People judge books by their cover, so make sure your cover says confidence and success.

#3 – The Mouth Piece: How to talk and communicate effectively for the best results every time. The way you use this tool can mean the difference between being broke and having a thriving business. This includes face-to-face, online and written communication.

Let's get to it.

CHAPTER 5
Tool #1 – The Mind

Everything you ever want to accomplish takes the right mental attitude. We think first, and then we do what we think about. Even if we never act on our first thought, we think we can't do something so we do just that, nothing. Thoughts turn into some type of action – and action gets us our results.

Thoughts + Actions = Results

Let's call this formula **"Mental Mathematics"**.

I remember when I was younger, around 10 years old; I used to take karate classes. This was mainly because I watched too many kung-fu movies but my parents figured I had to put my energy somewhere so they enrolled me.

I rose up in the ranks to a green belt (halfway between white belt and black belt in our system) and it was time for the AAU Martial Arts Competition in Atlanta, Georgia.

I lived in Denver, Colorado at the time but my parents came up with the money for me to go. I was to compete in two things. Forms (a single person going through moves as if they were fighting an opponent) and sparring (fighting another person, my favorite). My martial arts instructor spent the whole month preparing us on strategy and the rules of the competition. He taught us the knife-hand strike. This strike was to be used as sort of a "trick move" and its target was the opponent's back. If you landed this, you would get a full point. Three points and you win the match.

I felt I was ready. That was until I stepped into that building.

This place was huge! There were so many spectators that I couldn't even count them. It was a sea of people. There were hundreds of competitors all different ages, belts and weight classes. The floor where the martial artists competed was dead center stage. And suddenly I got a strange feeling. I felt like I was in over my head. I became nervous and my self-esteem plummeted.

It showed too. I completely messed up doing my forms. They were sloppy and showed no sharpness of technique. So, no medal there. My self-esteem dropped further.

It was also on this day that I was to spar. I wasn't ready. I competed before in competitions, but this was different. This was people from all over the United States! Maybe they knew something I didn't?

In all honesty, I was just ready to get my losing over with. So I waited for the sparring to start. And I waited and waited and waited. I don't know how many hours had passed but now I was just ready to get it over with. What was taking so damn long?

Finally it was my age and belt class up next. My instructor came and got me. He directed me to the mat and told me to do my best.

My first round. I got on the mat, looked at my opponent, bowed with respect and made it a point to get this over with as soon as humanly possible. I figured the best way for this to get over quickly was to "trick" him into exposing his back so I could land a couple knife-hand strikes. They were worth a full point so it would make this match lightning fast. That was the **thought**.

We began. I was moving, bobbing and weaving. I was throwing kicks to keep him at a distance and as soon as he got frustrated enough, he rushed in. Perfect! I side stepped and threw the knife-hand strike to his back. That was the **action**.

"Full point!" the judge said.

'Wow,' I thought, 'that was easy!' And I did it again. Another point. And I did it again. BAM! Another point. Match over. I won! I didn't think that would happen.

The competition went on and I carefully defeated opponent after opponent after opponent. Yeah I scored some points with punches and kicks, but the main tactic I used was my new technique – the knife-hand strike!

Rest of the story short, I beat every single one of my opponents – and I won the gold medal. When I got back to Denver the local newspaper, The Denver Post, coined me Colorado's Karate Kid. True story.

My strategy on properly using that knife-hand strike was what did it. And that was the **result**. A gold medal.

So again, the Mental Mathematics: Thoughts + Actions = Results

Mental Mathematics has never failed me, and it won't fail you either. Now let's dig into some important Game, principle by principle.

Principle 1: Acting Your Part

Every Hustler knows this! Whether they know it sub-consciously, or know it in application, they still use it. They understand that in order to go out in the world and do what they do, they must put on a mask. Confused?

You must realize that the world is truly a stage, and that we are all actresses and actors on it. When you get out there and Grind you are performing!

The reason for this is because your customers are buying from **you**. Sure they're getting their product or service in return for the money they're spending, but it's **you** that gives it a life. It's **you** that gives it a meaning. It's **you** that has the solution to their problem. **You** are their main point of contact.

I know you realize that your customers can more than likely get their product or service from somewhere else. But you want that money, right? So your job is to bring them from their world into yours. In your world, you're the star.

You're probably saying to yourself, that's a lot of pressure. It's not that serious, really. Most people fail to realize that they must create a separate role for themselves and then just act out their part. Follow me on this one. Let me ask you a question.

When you think of getting dressed up and going out on a date to get your favorite food, what comes to mind? The majority of the time it's one of your favorite restaurants. Now let me ask you why you go to this particular restaurant instead of the hundreds that are out there? It could be any number of reasons. Maybe you like the atmosphere, it could be the great quality of the food, it could be that it's closest to your house or maybe it's because they serve your favorite dish just the way you like it.

Another question.

What kind of soda do you drink? And if you don't drink soda, then what's your favorite beverage? And do you go look for a particular brand when you go shopping? You are loyal to a particular brand because you like the taste. And you know that every time you go buy that particular brand, you're going to get that same taste you like. You prefer *this* brand over *that* brand. Now what just happened? You have just left your world, and entered theirs. They become your problem solver.

You must make it a point in business to get people feeling the same way about you. You want them to say things like, "I prefer to buy from such and such because I like the way he or she does business," if a person likes the way you do things and feels they need what you sell, they will become a loyal customer. They will prefer spending money with you over someone else.

SIDE NOTE: I will be talking a lot about selling in this chapter and this subject frightens a lot of people. Some people hate the idea of selling anything. Point taken. Just be patient with me, all of this will come together near the end of this chapter. Proper selling is not what many of you have been taught it is.

So what is this mask that a Hustler wears? Well, it's the mask of his or her role in business. It's not about being fake or deceitful; it's simply about turning up the volume on a portion of your personality.

We all play different roles in our lives. We can be a son or daughter, a friend, a boss or employee, a husband or wife, a parent, a student and many other things all in the same day. Now, you wouldn't act like you act as an employee to your friends would you? And I bet you wouldn't treat your husband or wife like you would your boss, could we agree on that? These different roles that we play in life are just different parts of one personality – Yours!

We all do this every single day and do it with no effort. It's a natural habit.

So now we are going to create a new role for you to play in your life. This one will be used for business. If you already have one then read this anyway, perhaps I can give you a new idea or two.

We have four easy steps here that will help you to create this new role in your life.

STEP ONE: Relax and let's use our imaginations for a moment. Now put yourself in the shoes of a customer that is buying from the "business role", you. As you play this out in your mind watch what is taking place. How is the "business role" of you acting? How is this person dressed? Is he or she dressed in a suit and tie or casual, maybe even in jeans and a dress shirt? What is this person's personality like? Laid back and cool or cracking jokes and keeping you laughing?

The challenge here is simple – you must become the kind of person you, yourself, would buy from.

Who would you rather deal with? Someone who looks like they are in a good mood all the time, or pissed off? Someone who is helpful and caring about your needs or someone who looks like they are only about the money? Someone who takes care of their customers or someone who could care less about how their customers feel? Someone who is confident and knows their business in and out or someone who wouldn't even buy what they're trying to sell?

You must become that person you see in your mind. That is your role. And with this role, you can bring people into your world. The world is a stage and when you're doing business, the spotlight is on you. Remember that.

STEP TWO: Give this "business role" responsibility. What is this role accountable for? What is important while you're playing this role?

This is a very important concept. This image needs to stay clear in your mind. No different than when you're at your job. If you lose focus on this you may end up acting more like a friend then the business person you're supposed to. Remember when it's business time, you're in your business role. When it's friend time, you're in your friend role. This is not to say don't be friendly to your customers. You won't keep customers if you're a jerk. I'm just making a point, business first when it's time for business.

Whenever you lose focus and get off track, all you have to do is remember what your "business role" is responsible for. Let's make a list. Grab some paper and something to write with. It'll be quick I promise.

Some of the responsibilities you write down may look similar to this. Here is a part of my personal list:

- Take care of customer complaints quickly and to their satisfaction as much as possible
- To make "X" amount of money per month even if I have to work extra hard (*this is called a quota, we'll get to that later*)
- To make such and such number of new customers per week

- I will do my best to make all my appointments on time
- I will do my best to make all my deliveries on time
- I will not handle any personal business while I'm making money unless it's an emergency. That's an employee mentality, and I'm a boss
- Other people's bad attitudes and negativity will not affect me (when I'm in my business role, I stay there at all times)
- I will keep up to date with the latest information that affects my business and pass that on to my customers
- Regular customers will get special treatment because they earned it. But I am grateful for all my customers and I will let them know that

Easy right? If you can stay focused on these while you're in your "business role" you will be successful at it. It takes focus, commitment and discipline, but you have that, don't you?

STEP THREE: Give your new role a name. That's right, sounds silly doesn't it? But it will help you, trust me on this. You never have to tell other people this name if you don't want to, but when you're in business mode and you're talking to yourself in your head (like we all do), use it!

Say to yourself, "Hey such and such, only a few more sales for the day and you'll reach daily quota," or maybe, "You're allowing yourself to get distracted such and such, get back focused."

Now me personally, I tell all my customers to call me by this name. It's an immediate reminder every time I hear it to stay in my "business role". Just try it; you'll be convinced it works just by using it.

STEP FOUR: Learn to turn up the volume on this side of your personality. This is a formation of a new habit and new habits aren't easy to start. You need to make a serious effort for at least 30 to 45 days for this to stick with you. But when it does, it will be with you for the rest of your life. It will become so easy that you won't even have to think about it anymore. Just like you learned to act a certain way around your parents, learn to act a certain way in your business. Simple.

Principle 2: The Mindset – It's All About Attitude

You get out of something what you put into it. Garbage in, garbage out. Or as the saying goes, "What goes around comes around."

Do you seriously think you're going to succeed in business with a bad or negative attitude? If you piss off your customers do you really think they'll come back to you if they can get what you have from somewhere else?

"The amount of money you make is 75% the result of your attitude."
- W. James Dennis

Let me say it like this. Remember our Mental Mathematics formula?

Thoughts + Actions = Results

If you think negative, your actions will be negative and then your results will be negative. Negative attitude, negative results. Positive attitude, positive results. It's so simple that we usually forget about it.

The world can only give back what you put in. You could have the best location, the best product, the best price, etc. But you will never see your money the way you should see it with the wrong mindset. The word of mouth about your negative attitude alone will stomp out your business like Godzilla on Tokyo.

Life is truly cause and effect. If you know the causes then you can predict the effects. Look at this like a cake recipe. If you follow the recipe with serious attention to detail, then you should be able to bake the cake.

So what is the Hustler's attitude when it comes to business?

Before we dig into that I would like you to understand something. You must learn to think both long-term and short-term.

For short-term thinking you must concentrate on doing what every business must do. Get customers and secure clients. No cash flow and your business will not take off and will not grow. The Game is based around survival remember?

You must build clientele, it's your regular clientele that will secure your future in business and take you through those slow times. And those slow times will come trust me. You cannot successfully build clientele if you are lying and cheating them. Period. This should go without saying but I'm saying it anyway.

Your long-term thinking or should I say strategy, is to get yourself as far up the Money Chain as possible. To stop "owning a job" and actually having a business. If you have to constantly be at your office or place of business to make money, although you're self-employed, it's not much different than having a job. You will work harder in your own business than you ever will at a job.

You're ultimate goal is to put as much of your business on auto-pilot as possible. If you don't do this, you will find yourself jailed by your own business. You will have very little freedom, and that's what hustling is all about. Freedom! The freedom to do things, have time for loved ones and be able to take that vacation when you feel like it. Are you with me on this?

So what's the mindset we're talking about here? It's really a combination of many things but to simplify it I would say it's four main things.

(1) Reasonable Expectations – You must expect the best from yourself at all times. And you must expect the best results at all times. Even when things look their worst, you must refocus your mind on expecting the best. Keep a balance here though. Don't expect to make one-hundred thousand dollars in your first year of business and you have never run a business before (although things like this are possible, they're also extremely rare). That's just not realistic. Keep it real with yourself and always expect the best of what is in your power to do. Stay optimistic.

(2) Determination – Enough cannot be said about this attitude. The moment you give up is the moment you may miss the rewards of all your hard work. Now, will things always work out for the best? No. But you can't throw in the towel until there is nothing left to throw in *but* the towel.

Give your business venture everything you've got for as long as you possibly can. Effort pays off. Even if your business doesn't succeed to the bounds you wanted, the lessons you should have learned will still be worth more than any book or class could teach you.

(3) Be a Good Giver and a Good Receiver – People are generally better givers than they are receivers. Wealthy people are very good receivers. There was a period of time during my first months in business that it was hard for me to take people's money without me feeling slightly guilty. Now I'm like, "Give it HERE!" There's absolutely nothing wrong with receiving the rewards you've worked for.

When you do give, don't you feel good about it? How do you think people feel when they give to you? Don't deny them of the joy of giving. If you've worked for it and they give it to you of their own free will, then just except it and be grateful.

What goes around comes around, so give as much as you can in the way of good service and/or products. And when it's time for it to come back around, you will reap all the benefits and rewards. You cannot be selfish in business! After all you will be dealing with people and no one likes to deal with a selfish individual, especially if they're spending their money with them. I think this is self explanatory.

(4) You Must Create, Not Wait – Things will not just fall out of the sky into your lap. This is life in reality. You must, at all times, create situations for business to come to you. You must build your own roads and all those roads must lead to your business.

If you work a job, you're in the habit of waiting. You wait for a lunch break. You wait to get paid. You wait to get off from work. You wait for someone to acknowledge how special you are and give you a raise or promotion. You cannot have this mindset in business! If you wait, you will always be waiting. And you will wait yourself into a business flat line; dead on arrival.

Create, don't wait. In other words take action and stop being reactive. Be the force, the heart and soul of your business. Make sure people know about you and make sure they always get their money's worth. This is one of the biggest differences between an employee mindset and an entrepreneur mindset.

There's more to this mindset and attitude but as you continue to read through this book you'll begin to get the big picture. Make these four things a part of your new "business role" we talked about earlier. Remember people can do business with whoever they choose, make sure their choice is you.

Create a reputation so strong that your customers are proud to bring their friends and family to you. When you get to this point (depending on your type of business) you will be doing less work and making more money. Again, it's very simple; all you have to do is do it.

Principle 3: The "Trigger" of Motivation

You know, there are entire courses and seminars written to teach people how to get motivated and stay motivated. Some are good, some are just garbage information. You know what motivation is? It's simply staying in motion; moving.

A big saying of mine is, "Keep it moving." All I'm saying is don't stop on your way to your goal. Keep going, keep busting through obstacles. Don't let your negative mind stop you. Don't let family or friends stop you, don't let the so-called haters stop you either.

I learned about 70% of all my business knowledge on the streets. Now when I tell business owners this, most of them immediately look at me like I'm anything other than a business man. Well, why is that? Whatever their reason, I don't care about how they look at me. I'm self-employed, I'm a business owner and I enjoy both my work and my freedom of time.

If I listened to these so-called haters, I wouldn't be where I am today. Simple. I didn't let anything stop me from getting started, and I don't let anything stop me from continuing. The only thing that can stop me is me. And this holds true for you too.

If you have a problem staying motivated feel free to invest in some good books on the subject but if you want something simple and easy, here it is.

Find something that inspires you. For me it was music. There were certain songs by one of my favorite artists that I would listen to everyday before I opened up shop. This music would inspire me and put me into my business role. It released any negative energy, replacing it with the desire and drive to succeed for that day.

It may not be music for you. It may be a good movie. It may be an online article about someone who inspires you. It could be your favorite book. It could be your children or a family member that has always been encouraging.

When you find this "trigger", use it every day before you go out and do your business. Listen to those songs, read that article, watch that movie. If possible, talk to that person with those positive words for you or just keep a photo of them in your cell phone.

The key here is to start your day out on a positive note. And end your day on a positive note. Successful people even need to stay inspired and they waste no time to seek that out for themselves. Why should you do anything less?

While in your business role, don't let anything negative take you out of "character". People with negative attitudes are just a part of life. But we always have the choice whether or not to take in what they are dishing out. Choose not to. If you let someone take you out of your business role, then you need to work harder on making your business role more a part of you. Don't let anything drain your motivation. This takes practice and even I get distracted or pissed off sometimes, but I always get myself back on track in a few minutes. Find that "trigger" and use it, every day until one day, you won't need it as much anymore. It will take just a thought and you'll be ready to go.

Principle 4: The Importance of Proper Focus

Often times I'm asked, "Is being self-employed how you really make your living?" I smirk and respond positively. Some people even go on to say, "I just don't know how you do it." I respond, "It's just me. I'm happier when I'm steering my own ship."

This brings me to a point I'd like to make. When one is an entrepreneur, one cannot completely focus on making money. I hear you thinking, "What?" Just wait a moment, have some faith in me.

Yes and true, we set up a business to make money, but you can't just focus on money because you'll go broke chasing dollars. Sounds silly doesn't it? It's paradoxical. I learned this the hard way, when you are desperate for money and you really need it, you're more likely to stress yourself and come short of your goal.

What you focus on expands. With that in mind, if you're focused on coming up short on paying your bills, you're hustling out of desperation, and chances are you'll fail. That fear of not being able to pay your bills will dominate your mind. That becomes your focus, not on running your business well. And the focus on running your business well is where your focus should be at. But if you dwell on that fear, it will expand and it just may become the reality you will face.

When I started I made the stupid mistake of going all out with the last of what I had. I couldn't help it. I hated working a job with a passion. I figured it's now or never! So you know me, I jumped both feet in. This thinking put me in a squeeze though. I had to work harder and harder, and the more I worked the less money I made and the more frustrated I became. It's difficult to describe what this feels like inside. You feel like a failure. And guess what? You have to stuff those emotions inside of you and head out the next day to do it all over again. You're hustling out of fear – the fear of losing what you already have.

When you start your enterprise, always start with something in reserve for yourself. A cushion so to speak. Common sense you say? No, not really. Common sense isn't always a common thing. The point I'm making here is when you go to make your money, have a goal in mind, then just concentrate on doing the work for the work's sake. Sounds kind of Zen, wouldn't you agree? But from my experience it's a fact.

When you're focused and relaxed your energy flows and you will always end up in the right place at the right time. It's like magic. But when your energy is low and you are desperate, well let's just say you'll receive the results of that thinking. It's called "broke hustling". You're already broke, and you're trying to make money to keep yourself from hitting rock bottom. It's a lose-lose proposition. It should be like this – you have money in reserve, your needs are taken care of and you hustle to improve your situation further. Let that sink in for a moment.

Focus on doing the work, not on the money. If you do the work properly, the money will come. It's like fishing. You go at the right time, to the right area with the right bait, you're bound to come up with something.

Your focus should be your **"reason why"**. Why are you in business? I mean seriously. Are you trying to be more in control of your time? Perhaps you are Grinding to create a better lifestyle for your family? Maybe it's to have access to the finer things in life. Whatever your "reason why" is, let that be your goal. Let that help keep you motivated. If this reason is not strong enough, you will eventually throw in the towel way too soon.

Now with the overall goal in mind, you can then go on to just running your business. Do the best every day in your business, knowing that with each and every successful action (every single detail) you are on your way toward your overall goal.

If your "reason why" does not move you (remember moving is motivation), then you have the wrong reason.

Your reason should be one of the first things you think about when you wake up, and one of the last thoughts on your mind when you go to bed. It should be that strong. It should be that important to you.

Quick note here, human beings change, we grow and learn more. What was a strong enough reason for you last year, may not hold true for you this year. This is completely natural and there is no need to feel guilty about it. Just take your time to find your new reason why and use that.

Your reason why will take you from day to day, through good times and bad times, it will in essence, keep you moving (motivated). Find it, think about it often and visualize it. Then go do your work giving as much to it as possible.

No one can get something for nothing, the price you pay is running your business with everything you have in you. This is the payment for what you want out of your enterprise. I hope you truly understood what you just read. Remember our Mental Mathematics? Well it applies here.

Thoughts (Your overall goal/your reason why) **+ Actions** (The positive work you put into your business) **= Results** (The obtainment of your goal/reason why)

To further clarify, make an effort to make sure you do your best, every single time, no exceptions; your work should be consistent and reliable.

Let's go back to our cookie example from the Forward of this book. You would not cut any corners when baking those cookies. You would make sure each and every batch was made the same. You would use the best ingredients your money could buy every single time. Burnt cookies or the ones that were too small would not be sold at all.

Do you think a powerhouse such as Coca-Cola takes short cuts when they make their products? They can't afford to, their products must maintain a consistent taste. Take a cue from the Big Boys, why should you do anything less?

Principle 5: Selling Yourself and Selling Your Product or Service (in that order)

This is a simple principle to understand, but it takes a long time to master. We already covered it when we opened our first lock in Chapter Four. But it's so important that we need to go into more detail here.

It only takes about 10 seconds or less to make an impression on someone. This impression in made up of many things. Your posture, tone of voice, your hand gestures, the way you walk, the way you dress, the words you use and the way you use your eyes.

The biggest thing is trust. People have to like you and trust you even if they don't know you. Now, how is this accomplished?

We'll cover your appearance in the next chapter but for now you need to know that you must project a sense of confidence. Not a sense of shadiness, giving off the impression that you're not to be trusted.

Looking at this from a mental angle, your customer or prospect must "feel" you before you even say a word. This is accomplished mentally first. You must be genuine. You must sincerely have the desire to help them solve their problem. This must be true even if it means you won't make the sale. Just by holding this thought, it will change the way you present yourself to your customer.

You will be forward about what you're selling, but not pushy (although some pushing is necessary – we'll talk about that later). If you're there to help solve a problem and not push your product or service, people will feel that. This is hard to fake which is why I said you must be sincere. So to repeat again what we covered earlier – don't concentrate so much on selling a product or service. Concentrate on solving people's problem *with* your product or service.

Be the helper in your mind at all times. If your product or service matches what your customer needs then the sale is half way done.

"Sell them on the solution to the problem, not the product or service."
- W. James Dennis

Some say sell the sizzle, not the steak. When you do this, you aren't really selling at all. Again, you're just being helpful. Keep this in the front of your mind. In Principle Nine of this chapter I will deal with the dreaded fear people have of selling – the fear of rejection.

Principle 6: The Infamous Quota Principle

To help add to your focus (and your "business role") you need to develop a quota for yourself. It's a measuring rod that you'll use to make sure you're on track.

For those that don't know what a quota is I'll give you the non-dictionary definition. It's simply how much money you need to make per month to take care of your business and everyday living expenses (your needs, not your wants). If you have started your business part-time and are still working a job, then your business needs to be structured in such a way that you can get yourself out of the rat-race, as they call it.

Let's come up with your monthly quota. Grab some paper and something to write with, and if you're terrible in math like I am, grab a calculator too.

(1) Write down all your bills for the month:

Mortgage or rent, electric and/or gas bill, cell phone bill, internet service, car note, car insurance, health insurance, etc. (don't forget to add in your average grocery bill for the month as well).

Now add up that total.

(2) If you already have a business then also add in everything it costs to just break even, meaning no profit, just enough to keep the business running.

If it's hard to come up with a monthly total, then do it for the entire year and then divide that total by 12. This will give you a monthly total.

(3) Now add up both totals from steps one and two (If you don't currently have a business then you would only have the total from step one).

(4) Next multiply the total from step three by two (double it).

Write this total down and mark it as "Grand Total". This is approximately what you need to be making per month to take care of everything and still have a little breathing room.

Now a month is a long time. It's hard to truly gauge how well you're doing if we look at it from this far away, so let's get more specific shall we?

(5) Take the Grand Total from step four and divide it by four (for four weeks in a month). This will give us our "Weekly Grand Total". Go ahead and label it that.

(6) Now take this Weekly Grand Total and divide it by how many days you work your job and/or operate your business per week. The average of course is five or six days. This new total is our "Daily Grand Total".

To measure if we're living up to what we need to be doing for the month and year, we need to make sure we're hitting our "Daily Grand Total". If this is difficult, you should concentrate on hitting your "Weekly Grand Total" instead. The Daily Grand Total (or Weekly Grand Total) is our infamous quota. If you're hard core you can even go further and divide it so you have an hourly quota (most Hustlers do this). Just take your Daily Grand Total and divide it by how many hours you work or operate your business per day.

Why all this math? Well like I said, to help keep you focused. We multiplied our Monthly Grand Total by two because some of that money needs to be used to expand our business and make investments. Remember when we talked about "flipping" your money? Turning one dollar into three dollars? This is the foundation for actually having money to flip.

If our needs are taken care of and we have a little play money, it's much easier to put money aside to flip it. Your first goal of course is to make two times more than you need to take care of your living and/or business expenses.

To those of you stuck at a job, you may need to work a little over-time for a couple of months until you have the extra money to get your business up and running. Realistically you would have to work almost twice as much as you do now and that may not be possible. Don't worry! I will cover some math with you later that will show you how to properly save and budget the money you do have. If you're serious about getting into the Game, this shouldn't be a problem for you.

For now just realize that one of your first goals is to make **twice** as much as you need. If you already do that then great! If not then study, *'A Business from Nothing'* section carefully in Chapter Nine.

Keep this number in your mind at all times. Trust me, there's a great high that comes when you realize that you are hitting your quota. That feeling of, "I made this happen!"

We'll go deeper into this subject later so put those numbers somewhere so you can find them. And here's something for you to think about – the money you need is already out there, you just have to go get it. This is part of the proper mindset. Remember to create, not wait.

Principle 7: The Secret Behind the Magnetic Personality

Have you ever met someone that has the type of personality that just lights up the room? They seem almost stress free and they command attention although they don't go actively seeking it. They seem to get along with everyone and when they speak everyone seems to listen to what they have to say.

I remember years ago when I was just getting the hang of business, one of my hustling partners and part-time mentor was a little low on money. It had been a rough month for him. Let's call him Burns. Now Burns was the type of guy who could literally sell ice to an Eskimo. He realized he had gotten a little lazy in his business and was determined to get himself back on track.

We had gotten up early that particular day and met with our wholesalers. After getting what we needed we were off to our outdoor vending location where we would set up shop for the day.

It was hot! I mean scorching outside. It was summer time and anyone that knows what Georgia heat feels like will know immediately what I'm talking about.

Anyway, we set up shop and began to work. Burns outside of work was always very friendly and you rarely caught him in a bad mood, but when it was time to work he hit a zone where you just couldn't stop him. People were just drawn to him. Here he was making sale after sale after sale and I was maybe making one out of every 10. Needless to say I was getting discouraged. But Burns was on fire and it wasn't from the outdoor heat!

We didn't want to be outside too long because of the blazing sun but we both had our quota and we wanted to make it as quickly as possible. Well Burns made his quota in less than an hour. And he proceeded to triple his quota in a little over two hours. For me it took three whole hours to make quota. By that time Burns was almost out of stock and was helping me sell off my inventory. Almost everyone he talked to came over just to see what he had, and almost everyone bought something.

After we were done for the day he could see the frustration in my eyes, I guess it was written all over my face. I mean we worked together so how could I hide the fact that it took me forever to get in gear? He looked at me and said, "It's a vibe man, you just have to catch it." And these words still stick with me to this day.

What did he mean by that? He meant that you can literally magnetize people to you. He was creating, not waiting. He built rapport just by putting out more energy (the right kind of energy) than everyone else around him, including me. He worked with the very spirit of what we were doing. Let me put a scenario in front of you.

Let's say you're at the beach. It's hot and of course most people are dressed in swimwear. But here comes this guy, he's dressed in a three piece suit and tie. The suit is an ugly green color and he has on dress shoes with matching socks as well. Now, just by looking at him you would think he was a fool. Does he even know where he's at? People are laughing and pointing at this idiot but it doesn't seem to bother him.

He walks up and down the beach waving at people, giving high fives to kids and generally seems to be enjoying himself. He's opening up conversations with person after person. When he's through talking to a particular person or group they seem to be generally very happy he stopped to talk with them, and as he continues to walk he finally approaches you.

"Hello!" He says with a slight smile. He's cheerful but not annoyingly so. He continues, "Great day here at the beach isn't it? I would love to go for a swim but I forgot my swim trunks. Shame on me!"

He chuckles a little and then some children run up to him laughing as they kick sand on him. He playfully kicks some back. The young kids scream and yell wildly running off laughing louder and he laughs too.

"So, what brings you here today?" He asks you. You here a faint ring. Yep, it's definitely his cell phone. He takes it out of his pocket and answers it.

"Hey! Oh, really? Alright well give him whatever he wants. Eight million dollars? Whoa! That's a little steep but go ahead and have his lawyer fax us the contracts. I don't care how much it costs. Just get it done. Thanks Claudia. Bye."

He turns back to you and says, "Oh, sorry, let me introduce myself. I'm George Anderson and I'm a real estate investor. I was thinking of buying up about a dozen square blocks of commercial property here and just wanted to know how often you come to this beach and what do you like most about it? I want to improve the area, but not take away the things that people find charming."

Has your perception of this man changed? At first he was a fool in a three piece suit now he's a multi-millionaire real estate tycoon with a bad taste in clothes. Because of your change in perspective, would you alter the way you talk to this man? Be honest, of course you would. And why? Because he's not an idiot or a fool, he's a serious man with a serious goal in mind.

The point of this story is this, the way people perceive you can change when they realize you are in a position of **perceived** power. I say perceived because you may not actually be in a position of power at all, but if you are giving off that "vibe" or energy, people will fall in line with it. You must align yourself with the very essence of this perceived power.

When people perceive that you are in control of the situation and you look and sound like you know what you're doing, they will relax around you, and also open up to you. It's just the way human beings have been conditioned.

The key word here is confidence. Confidence is like a flame, it warms and soothes.

A person, who is confident about what they say and what they do, even if others disagree with it, will naturally garner respect. This vibe is like a magnet and it draws people to you; right into the flame.

The more you know about your business and your product or service and the more confident you are when you tell people about it, the more they will (in their mind) separate themselves from you. This works to your advantage. They will look at you as an expert, or at least as someone who knows more about the subject than they do.

If you can project this confidence and knowledge in a laid-back and friendly way, people will respond to it. The key is to pull them in, not push it on them, a very important distinction.

My dear readers, an expert in a field or industry is not the person who knows *everything* about the subject; an expert is just someone who knows more about the subject than the person he or she is talking to.

This vibe is simply confidence in the way you speak and present your product or service. It is the way you make your customer or prospect an expert also by sharing what you know. You should share with them as much as they want to know. Again pull them in, don't push it on them. People naturally respond and relax around people like this, and of course this is what you want.

This subject is very in depth and I don't have room to go into a lot of detail here. But it's very important to learn how to correctly communicate with people and to know everything you can about your business. The rest is all about being friendly, helpful and open to the person you're talking to. In return, they'll open up to you.

Principle 8: Creation - Why Competition Shouldn't Drive Your Business

You know what's funny? When I used to study all those business books most of them always reinforced the idea of competition.

Everyone wants to learn how to crush the competition. "Business is a dog eat dog world!" *they* say. And they also spend about 40% of their time, money and resources figuring out how to do that. It's a waste of time, money and resources. The Game is survival and going to war when it's not warranted is a violation of the Game. It hurts your business more than it hurts your opponents. Let me explain.

Business, like any type of sport, is naturally competitive. But you don't need to compete or crush your adversaries to be successful. The higher you go up on the wealth ladder the less competition there is. It's hard to get to the top and even harder to stay there so this means less people to compete with. That's what *they* say anyway.

The very idea of competition immediately puts you in a frame of mind that you don't measure up. You must be as good, if not better than your competition in order to make a dime. But when you start with this mindset you immediately put yourself in a place of defense rather than offense. And the ideas this generates move you further and further away from being unique and creative. As a small business being unique works to your advantage, why hinder yourself?

In most sports, defense is great and it's necessary to keep the other team from scoring. But you cannot score anything yourself if you do not have offense.

You must learn to think in terms of creating, not competing. Focus more on scoring than on how to keep the other team down. Again I ask do you know what Game you're playing?

When you think in terms of there being competition you are in a state of fear. You are afraid there isn't enough to go around. You are afraid that the next woman or man is better. You are afraid that if you don't beat your competition to that customer then your business will fail. Do you see my point? How can you be successful if you operate out of fear?

The mind that thinks in terms of competition is full of doubt, worry, fear and stress. Who wants to live like that? I don't.

Remember when we talked about proper focus in Principle Four? Well that applies here. If you're focused on the idea that there's not enough to go around, then that's what you'll get out of your business. That thought will shape your actions and then shape your results (Mental Mathematics). Your results will then not be on making your business better for the sake of the business itself, it will instead be on making your business better so you look better than the "other business". A Hustler (who is not at "war") does not compete, we create. A Hustler learns to maneuver through dark corridors with no flashlight. They have a natural sense of direction.

What's creation? It's the mindset that we will do everything we can with what we have. We know there's plenty to go around and we know that people will always make a choice. Some will choose us, some won't. We're not worried about those that don't; we're more concerned about those that do. We live by the principle that there is plenty to go around; all we have to do is go get it (or set up a situation where it comes to us). We make sure our business runs well because we want it to reflect us. We don't run our business well to look better or equal to "them".

Do we ignore the fact of competition? Not at all, business is competitive after all. But we just don't let what **they're** doing affect what **we're** doing. We create our business to be the best because that's what we want. We know what goes into something, comes back out. We don't put the idea of fear in there.

We welcome competition because it helps us stay sharp and gives us ideas on how to run our business more efficiently. We humble ourselves to recognize that they can teach us a thing or two. But when it comes down to it, we have a vision for our enterprise and we create just that, our vision.

As you continue reading this book you'll run across more concepts and ideas that fall into this mindset principle. This simple change of perspective will keep a lot of stress off you, so make it apart of your business role.

Principle 9: The Law of Average –What Selling is and What It's Not (How to Sell Without Selling)

I hear this a lot when I tell people that I started my business by selling face to face. "I don't think I could do that. I HATE selling!" they say. When I ask why, they may give a few reasons here and there but in the end it just boils down to one main thing. People only hate selling because they have a fear of rejection. They hate hearing the word, "No".

Some people take the word very personally. Some professional sales instructors say this stems from the fact that when we were kids we were told, "No!" by our parents over and over again. It was mainly said when we were doing something our parents didn't approve of, or when they refused to give us something we wanted.

So over the years the word stuck with us and we associate it with being bad or being rejected. Interesting theory, it's a good starting point, but I think we can pull back another layer of this onion.

People don't like hearing the word no because they associate it with being a failure. And who likes feeling like a failure?

Some women are masters at this. If they find themselves interested in a man, they will very seldom approach him in a straight forward manner. They are afraid of being rejected. They are afraid that they just may not be good enough or attractive enough to gain the interest of that man. So what do these women do? They drop hints, do subtle flirting and laugh at his corny jokes in hopes that he will get the hint, "Hey, I'm interested in you. I'm open for some more in depth conversation or maybe a date!" Some men go through the same game with women that they find attractive as well. The fear of rejection is universal.

So just what is rejection really? It's simply the belief that you just aren't good enough. You just don't have what it takes. You're a failure or a loser.

If you have this belief in you, you are going to have a hard time getting your business up and running properly. Understand Game – **nothing happens until something is sold**. You must sell sooner or later or nothing will happen in your business (except it shutting down faster than you set it up).

Let's go back for a moment to our example of our favorite beverage. You prefer one brand over the other, right? Well aren't there people who don't like the brand you drink and prefer another one? Do you think the companies that make these beverages really care who likes what they make and who doesn't? For the most part no, they are more focused on pleasing the people who do like their product and attracting new people who have never tasted it.

Now if someone comes to you and says they don't like what you drink do you take that personal? No, you don't, why should you? You like what you like and they like what they like. The apples and oranges theory – some people are apple people. They like apples. Some people would rather have an orange. It's just human nature, we all like different things. There are even people who like both apples and oranges and also there are people who hate them both and just want a banana.

If someone doesn't want what you have to sell and says no, it is no different than when you make a decision to get one brand of juice over another. They may prefer to get the product or service elsewhere. You can't be upset at that, can you? They may not even be thirsty, meaning they are not "in the market" for what you're selling at the time. They don't need it. How can you take that personally?

These people are not rejecting you; they are just not interested in what you are selling at the moment (the apple). This may change (they may become interested later) or it may never change (they want an orange). It could even be the fact that they don't have enough money to spend at the moment.

When someone says, "No thank you," all they are saying is they are not interested *right now*. That's all. They are not saying you are a loser or that you're not good enough. You actually have very little to do with the equation.

Ever try to figure out what to give a crying baby to keep them quiet? You hand them a toy, they put it down and cry, you hand them a pacifier, they spit it out and cry, you figure maybe they're hungry; nope they spit that out too. Maybe their diaper needs changing, nope all dry. Hmmm, what could it be then? So you pick them up and they slowly relax and the crying stops.

Now when you were trying to figure out what this baby really wanted and they rejected your ideas, did you take that personally? Well no, you say, it's just a baby. And I say, what's the difference when you try to sell your product, service or idea in the market place?

People have many different types of problems. You only need to find the people who have the problem you can solve. If the people are "crying" for what you're selling, they'll let you know, if not, then you have the wrong thing for them, that's all. Again, you have very little to do in the equation.

As you ask people to buy from you all you are doing is finding out who really needs what you have to offer. You are eliminating all the people who don't have that particular problem. They are actually saving you a lot of time by telling you no. And time is money, isn't it? This process is called **qualifying**. Who is qualified to need or want what you have? If they do not have the problem you have the solution for, they are not qualified to be sold to. You would be wasting your time on them. We'll go into more detail about qualifying in a later chapter. But as you can see, it's not hard to figure out.

So next time someone tells you, "No," say thank you and mean it. Thank them for saving you precious time so you can move on to the next person who just may need what you have to solve their problem.

We have covered this over and over again so one more time. Selling has nothing to do with selling the product, service or idea itself. All you are doing is helping people solve their problem. If you have a solution to their problem then let them know.

"Selling? I don't sell anything. I just offer a solution to a problem for a good price in an interesting way."
- W. James Dennis

If you stop at a no, you will never get to a yes. Period. Remember you are a helper and make sure the customer knows that fact.

Selling is not pushing a product, service or idea. Selling is finding people with a problem and giving them a solution for a good price. Simple. Forget all that other crap, it only complicates things.

In our modern world, the root of the issue is trust. Why should a stranger trust you? Understand Game – Building trust should be the first priority. And as you build trust you are actually selling. But it is not your product or service you're selling; you're really selling yourself and your brand. Amazing how that works, isn't it?

Now on to the **"Law of Average"**.

This law states that: "If you have a single cause with multiple possible effects, over a given period of time, the effects will begin to even out."

To make it simple let's look at a coin toss. If you toss a coin in the air and record the number of times it lands on either head or tails you will find over a certain number of tosses, the results will just about even out.

Same thing in business. If you are out amongst the right kind of people, qualified people (people that have the problem you have a solution for) and you offer the solution to them they will say either "yes" or "no", heads or tails. Over a given period of time, the "yeses" and "no's" will even out.

Let's stop here a moment. Now when we say, "over a given period of time," we are talking in terms of months or years, depending on what you're selling.

Don't be discouraged! If you master this material, you'll be in business long enough to experience this for yourself. All we need in the beginning is to find these qualified people and make them the offer. People who do not qualify as needing our solution do not count.

Once we have our qualified people we make them the offer on our product, service or idea and we then have to humble ourselves to the Law of Average. Some people are going to say yes and some will say no. That's just how it is, it's in the numbers. The more qualified people we can offer to, the better chances we have of getting our "yeses".

To get an idea of how this works, and you have a business that you can keep track of sales numbers, grab a book of matches. There are 20 matches in a book. As you are out there Grinding and you find a qualified person (qualified people only) and make them an offer, for every no you get, take out a match from the book and throw it away. For every yes you get from a qualified person leave a match in the book.

After you have made your offer to 20 qualified people, count the number of matches still in your match book. This will give you your average. So if you have two or three matches left in the book, your average is two to three sales for every 20 qualified people you talk to.

You will notice that sometimes you'll have more than 10 matches left in the book. Sometimes you will have none. Sometimes your book will be almost full. Like I told you, if you're talking to qualified people, your result will eventually even out (depending on your business).

If you go through three matchbooks (60 people) and only have three or four "yeses", don't get down on yourself. You will find that maybe the next three matchbooks you go through will only have three or four matches taken out for the "no's".

Now before I bore you to death let me wrap this up.

Have you ever recommended a restaurant to a friend? How about a movie? Maybe you've recommended a trustworthy mechanic to someone who needed one? We do things like this very often and do not consider this selling. We consider it only giving good advice or being helpful. But you know what? This is exactly what selling really is at its core. And that's all.

So the next time you get all uptight and nervous about telling people what you sell (offer) or what you're business is all about, simply tell them how you solve a particular problem and you will reach more people in a genuine way then just by pushing it on them. Simple, isn't it?

Principle 10: Reputation

I will keep this brief. All the principles you have just read in this chapter all are focused on building yourself a solid reputation by keeping your mind focused on proper work ethic.

In order for your business to thrive, your business as well as yourself, must have an unshakable positive reputation. Trust is a huge issue, remember? A reputation takes a long time and a ton of consistent effort to build, but it can be crushed almost overnight. It's the expensive vase that holds the delicate flower. It can hold up under a few very minor cracks and blemishes, but once it is shattered there isn't much you can do about it.

If you recall, near the beginning of this book we talked about delivering. You must learn to deliver. Keep this in the foremost of your mind because this is what builds a solid reputation.

You're in business to solve problems, so solve the damn problems you claim you can solve!

No one respects someone who does not consistently keep their word. In business your word is your bond, break this bond at your own risk. By delivering regularly your reputation will build on its own with no further effort on your part. You will be known for doing what you do very well. Your customers will be satisfied and they will spread the word about your good work. The rewards of a good reputation are first compounded, and then multiplied.

The most important lesson I want you to take from this principle is this – **The way you start, is the way you have to finish**. Do not begin at a pace you can't keep up. Make an effort to under-promise and over-deliver whenever possible. If you can't over-deliver then just deliver what you initially promised. Either way, you win. You kept your word and that is what building an unshakable positive reputation is all about. That is some business Game for you to ponder on.

CHAPTER 6
TOOL #2 – The Body

A lot can be said about appearance. This is an important key because unfortunately people still judge others by their outward appearance. The way you look, move and dress will make an impression long before you open your mouth. This is just the way it is and you have to learn to use this to your advantage.

Although this tool is not as important as the mind (or the mouth piece for that matter), by looking your part, you will find people are initially more receptive to listen to you.

As we go through these principles, adjust them to your business and add them to your "business role". The way you dress is also another trigger to get you and keep you in character.

Principle 1: The First Impression – How to Put Together the Right Look

Appearance is very important, but not the most important thing. There are plenty of successful entrepreneurs out there who don't put too much effort into having the best, top of the line clothing or business attire and are doing just fine in business.

Is it more important for your business to shine with quality and professionalism then it is for you as an individual? Both are crucial, but your business takes priority.

You must dress well, but it doesn't take a fortune to do so. And depending on your business you could literally be spending peanuts (as they say) to get your look together.

The best of the Hustlers dress a certain way. It's very simple, they dress like their customers. This allows them to sort of blend in with those around them. When people perceive (there's that word again) that you're one of them, they will be more comfortable around you. You are relatable, not intimidating.

There are exceptions to this rule of course. If you are in a professional service business then your look needs to reflect professionalism. You must differentiate yourself from your customer because you must be perceived as the expert. Think real estate agent or insurance agent.

If your customers are in the corporate world, dress in the best suits, shoes and ties you can afford. If you own a local family restaurant where the atmosphere is fun and relaxed, you could get away with dressing in nice casual wear. A simple pair of khaki pants, some nice casual shoes and a pique polo shirt. Again, dress like your customers.

Been to a fast food restaurant recently? How do the employees dress? They dress very casual, relying more on colors then overall style. Why? Because how would it look if you walked up to the counter and the person taking your order was dressed in a pair of jean shorts and an old white t-shirt? Doesn't that just feel out of place?

Like I mentioned in the last chapter, it takes 10 seconds or less to make a first impression so let your appearance speak for you until you can say something out of your mouth.

Basic grooming and hygiene is a must. Keep your hair nicely done, your nails trimmed or manicured. Keep your attire clean and pressed. Keep your shoes clean. Wear pleasant smelling colognes or perfumes but just enough so that only people close to you can smell it. Keep your jewelry to a minimum, unless of course flaunting your jewelry falls in line with your type of business.

Your goal here is simply to look your best with what you have. People will notice. You can even search the web for deals on clothes or visit your local discount clothing stores that sale name brands that have been overstocked.

Keep your vehicle clean, inside and out, ensure it smells good inside. You may not have the best vehicle, but if you take care of it people will notice that. This translates in a person's mind sub-consciously. You take care of your appearance which means you pay attention to detail. If you take care of details like this, you probably take good care of your business as well.

Look like you're doing well and people will think you're doing well. That's just how we as human beings perceive things. Even if you're not doing so well, look like it. Another reason for this is because you never know when a great business contact or opportunity will come your way. If you already have your appearance together, you have one less hurdle to jump over when it comes to quickly establishing a sense of trust.

Police dress like police. Pastors or clergymen dress like pastors and clergymen. Doctors dress like doctors. Fast food workers dress like fast food workers. Would you mistake a fast food worker for a police officer? No! Why? Because they are dressed in a way that shows what business and/or industry they are in. So you should do the same. Look well, act well and people will perceive you to be doing well.

Principle 2: Flair - Also Known As the Art of Movement

Since we're on the subject of first impressions, it's very important to realize that the way you move, walking, your hand movements, the way you make (or don't make) eye contact, the way you smile, the way you stand, the way you sit and so on all adds to the 10 seconds or less time frame for making your first impression.

A person must like you first in order to trust you. This is the reason first impressions are so important. A certain level of trust must be established for someone to do business with you. Do you follow that?

Flair, meaning the way you move, says a lot of things about a person. It's what many people call body language. There are many books on the subject and I suggest going out to get one. In the meantime I'll give you some basic pointers to get you going in the right direction.

Flair is picked up by people on a sub-conscious level. They are not focused on your movements, but they do influence the way a person looks at you. If you feel that you don't have any flair, then you must develop it. Here are three things you can work on to improve your flair.

(1) Walking and Standing – Do me favor and stand up for a moment. Now put your feet about shoulder with apart. Look directly forward. Now bring your shoulders slightly back so that your chest moves forward while your arms naturally fall at your sides. To make sure you have this right take a deep breath and exhale.

If you did this correctly you will find that when you take that breath in, your stomach will expand as well as your chest. You can place one of your hands on your stomach to feel this happen. This is proper posture. This posture radiates confidence. Slumped over shoulders on the other hand says that you are either tired or have low self-esteem.

Now while you're in the proper posture walk around a little. Walk at a normal pace and just see how it feels. Don't do this all stiff and rigid, you'll look like either a robot or Frankenstein. Just let your arms swing naturally with each step and breathe normally as you walk. This is a walk of someone who is confident. Police officers use a similar method to give people the impression that they have authority.

Now return to a regular standing position. Let your knees slightly bend. You can then shift your weight to one foot. Not all your weight but enough to where you feel it.

Practice these and let them become natural for you. At first you'll be stiff and feel like an idiot but as you relax with them and blend them with how you walk and stand currently, they will become a part of you.

(2) The Eyes – You must learn to make eye contact with people who you are talking to. Again this shows a sense of confidence.

There is a big difference between staring someone down, and making good solid eye contact. Don't look like a psycho! You don't have to stare, just make eye contact.

When you look at someone, look into their eyes until you feel they are looking back into yours. Then refocus your eyes to the bridge of their nose. Since most people watch a person's mouth as they speak, a large percentage of people won't realize your subtle change in focus. As you are continuing to hold a conversation with this person, occasional focus back to their eyes and look into them. Make this contact briefly, a split second, from time to time.

All of this radiates self confidence and assurance. It also sub-consciously builds trust in the person you're speaking with.

3) Arms and Hands – Now me, when I'm really into what I'm talking about, my hands are moving around a lot and I am very animated. I had to learn to be very aware of what I was doing.

Too much hand and arm movement is not necessarily a good thing when you are meeting someone for the first time. In fact it's best to make as few arms and hand movements as possible. Quick note here, once the person shows comfort around you, it's fine to loosen up and be yourself. This is just for the initial first few minutes of conversation. Again, don't be a robot!

To force yourself to do this, let your hands naturally relax at your sides. While standing in this manner, you are more likely to use head and shoulder movements which are better at this point.

Some people suggest that you never cross your arms up near your chest when you're talking to someone. This gesture gives off the impression that you're stand-offish and closed to what they're talking about. I on the other hand use this every so often when I really don't want to make even the slightest hand or arm gesture.

These are the basics. Another technique is to slightly lean in toward the person you're talking to. This shows that you are giving them your full attention.

One more important point, learn to slow down. This is very important. Slow down your hand and arm movements. Slow down your walk. Slow down how fast you speak. If you decide not to use any of the other techniques I've just taught you, you will do yourself a huge favor by just slowing down. This alone shows confidence and rapport. This conscious effort of slowing down is the essence of developing flair. Slow deliberate movements and a nice even tone in your voice. Try it out for yourself and practice it. You'll be surprised how this makes you just feel more confident. And this feeling will be passed on to the person you're speaking with. Even over the phone it radiates like the light of the sun. Don't forget to smile.

CHAPTER 7
TOOL #3 – The Mouth Piece

This happens to be one of my favorite subjects when it comes to talking about the tools of Hustling. Not that it's more important than having the right mindset, because it's not, but it's a lot of fun to talk about (and now write about). The way you speak and the words that come out of your mouth (or in writing) make a big difference in getting the results you want out of life. Communication is a bridge, connecting you to someone else.

I guess one of the main reasons I enjoy talking about this subject is because when I was younger I had a very hard time talking to people. Even when I got into high school I still had this problem. This problem included talking to both adults and people around my age.

I felt nervous around new people. I simply didn't know what to say or how I should act. I used to watch my friends and they could start up a conversation with complete strangers, and at the time the most important strangers were young ladies.

The inability to communicate effectively is yet another way to show a lack of confidence. If you are not sure of the words that you speak, people will pick up on it. This lack of confidence and inability to know what to say can cause you to miss opportunities. A Hustler does not like to miss **any** opportunities. It would take me years to realize the cold hard truth that in business missing an opportunity is a violation of the Game. You're suffocating your business and hurting its odds of survival. Knowing how to talk to people is an essential skill, both in your regular life and in your business life.

Let's cover some principles.

Principle 1: Don't just Show Something, Say Something
Some Hustlers are all about being seen. "Look what I got!", "Look what I'm doing!", "I have this and this and do this! Please listen to me!" That's fine up to a certain point, you need to get people's attention whether verbally or in writing but you shouldn't waste time talking to people who don't want or need what you have. And how do you save this precious time? You need to find out

what the potential customer needs first. In other words, learn when to shut your mouth and let them speak.

Remember, your job is to simply give the people what they want. And make sure it's the right people. Whenever you enter a sales situation you have to remember this.

So try to make it a habit to "show" and then "tell" if that's possible in your business. Stay open, learn to ask the right questions so you can narrow the field down and find out exactly what they're interested in.

Let's look at this from Michael the Hustler's point of view. If you remember, he sells T-Shirts (Tee's). Michael would display his shirts so they can easily been seen and would also make an effort to let people know he has them. What is Michael looking for when he does this? He's looking for a **"SOI"** – a **Show of Interest**.

If you tell people you have something and they ask a question, this means they have an interest in what you're saying. People only ask questions if they are interested. That opening question they ask is a **SOI**.

What's next? Once a person indicates a **SOI** (show of interest) it is then time to qualify them. Qualification is simply discovering if you can solve your potential customer's problem. Would Michael immediately try to sell his shirts? No he wouldn't, he would return their question with a question. Something similar to this –

Person: Are you selling these shirts?

Michael: Yes I sure am. Are you looking for some Tee's today?

Person: Yeah… I was looking for something for my son.

Michael: Oh really? Excellent. How old is your son?

Person: He's 15; he loves these kinds of shirts.

Michael: These shirts are in style right now. What size does he wear?

What Michael is doing is asking a question to qualify this person. Again all that means is that he's trying to find out if he can solve this person's problem.

The best way to do that is to get to the root of the problem. If things match up, then Michael would go into actually selling the Tee, not before.

Let's look at another situation. Again Michael has set up shop and is selling his Tee's.

Person: Hey! How much are those shirts?

Michael: What style of shirts are you looking for today?

See what happened there? The customer went straight to the price but Michael still goes on to qualify the person before starting to sell.

This technique is called a "Return to Sender". It's a way of qualifying someone through the right questions and we'll go into more detail later in Chapter Nine.

Now let's say after all the qualifying is done and the customer seems interested enough to actually spend money, that's when Michael would begin to show his product in detail. The quality of it, the difference in designs, etc. By doing things this way, he saves a lot of time by not pushing the product first. He shows the product (or displays it), looks for those who are interested in what he has (they give a **SOI**), he then qualifies them and if there is a match, he goes into the sell.

Here's a recap:

(1) Show or display your product, service or idea (verbally, in writing, online, with a flyer, with pictures, with a brochure, etc.) to any and everyone who will listen.

(2) Ignore those that are not interested and look for those who give a **SOI**.

(3) Qualify the person who gives a **SOI** and make sure you can solve their problem.

(4) If you can solve their problem, then proceed to sell it to them.

We'll get into more detail about these steps later. Again this whole process can actually be done in writing if you're clever enough to put it together. The people who you can help will see the potential in your words and will qualify themselves.

Again the point to remember now is simply – help them find what they want. And you do that by asking questions in such a manner that you can get specific answers.

Principle 2: Using Proper Terminology

When it comes to using your mouth piece you also have to learn to use words in such a way that you don't feed negative emotions into the sale. It is very possible to talk (or write) your way right out of a sale. Let me explain about how to prevent this.

All words have meaning behind them and to complicate matters, many people have negative ideas or images associated with certain words. It's not about speaking superficially and ultra professional; it's simply about choosing certain words properly. You must replace words that have negative emotions or feelings behind them with words that don't.

What comes to your mind when I say the word "bills"? As in those things that come to your mailbox that you need to pay. Unless you're already very wealthy I bet you have some type of negative feeling or image attached to this word.

What if I say the word "depression"? What comes to your mind? Nothing positive I'm sure. How about the word "sex"? A little more positive?

Now, just like you, everyone has images and feeling associated with certain terms. You must learn to use your mouth piece in such a way that you remove the negative and place in the positive.

Using this principle properly can make you that breath of fresh air in their day. You can become that little ray of sunshine in the dark clouds of their mind. And all this takes very little effort once you get the hang of it. The reward of this action is two-fold. (1) People will remember you (even if they forget your name). And (2) People will become very comfortable around you. They will look forward to seeing you and speaking with you.

What does all this mean? It means you will make an impression in their minds. And that impression may lead to sales. Not just now, but also in the future. And that's what we want. When you make this impression you are putting yourself into the customer's mind. Add in a good attitude, a sharp appearance and some flair and BAM! You'll be hard to forget.

If you don't do anything else, at least get the words "sell" and "price" out of your vocabulary when you're talking to customers. Why? Because they usually have negative feelings and images associated with them. The word sell is a killer, people do not like to be sold.

Here is a short list of replacement words you can use as you sharpen your vocabulary and terminology:

- Don't say **price**! Use the word **total**, you can also say **"for only"**. Example: Michael would say that he is letting his t-shirts go "for only" ten dollars each.

- Never say **sell**! Use the word **offer** or the phrases – **"what I have"** or **"here is what is available."**

- Why tell your customer that you are adding another monthly **bill** to their lives? Use **payment, installment** or **monthly plan** instead. Yes we all know these mean yet another monthly bill, but it sounds just a touch nicer, doesn't it?

- You are not a **salesperson** – you are an **owner, associate** or **customer service representative**.

- You are not fulfilling a customer's **want** – you are fulfilling a customer's **need**. This is a re-frame. Example: Michael knows people **want** new t-shirts, but they **need** the latest styles and the best quality for their money. They deserve that after all, don't they?

- Avoid saying **"I don't"** or **"I can't"** – If there is any chance that you can or may be able to, say instead that you will see if you can **"get it"**, **"do it"** or say you will **"take care of it"**. Be careful here, remember you must always deliver on your word.

- You are not **"working on it"** – Just say that, **"it is processing"** or **"being done"**. Another re-frame. Working on something means, "work". Work is something time consuming, painfully unpleasant or a chore to finish.

I could go on and on but I think you see my point here. Two more things – First and foremost speak as if you are in control of the situation at all times.

Even if you're not. If someone assumes you are in control, it allows them to remain comfortable around you.

Secondly, avoid talking down to your customers. Don't make them feel as if they're not important and that you could care less what they have to say. This can even be done by using terms and words that specifically apply to your industry. Not everyone speaks industry lingo! Speak normally. Be careful not to get ahead of who you're speaking with. You will lose their attention.

For instance, if what you do is HTML 5 web design, only the most educated of computer geeks are going to understand you. Don't talk down to your customers or make them feel as if they don't know something. For the average non-computer geek you would just say, "I design websites that are smooth, run well and aren't plain and boring."

If you're talking to someone who knows the terminology of your industry then great! In that case, talk like you know what you're talking about. But if you're not talking to someone who's familiar with your industry, then keep it simple.

Remember, people just want solutions to their problems; they could care less how you use big words or terms. Tell them what they're getting in a way they understand and you will gain their trust and quite possibly their business. If you must use big terms then make it a point to explain exactly what you mean by them.

Principle 3: Getting People Open – Conversation Starters

I'll make this brief. There will be times when you must approach people to get your **SOI** (show of interest) from them. In order to do this you need to know how to "open them up", so to speak. The best and easiest way is simply to get them into a conversation.

In order to start a conversation you can focus on one of three main subjects:

(1) The person you're talking to
(2) Yourself
(3) The situation

Let's break this down. To start a conversation with anyone you can make a comment or ask a question about any of the three subjects above. Asking a question is the best way to go because it causes the person to give more information. The key here is to ask an "open-ended" question. An open-ended question is a question that cannot be answered with just a yes or no; it must be answered with some detail. You also want to avoid questions that people can give one word answers to. Let's look at a few examples:

What kind of cookies do you like?
What do you think your sister is doing right now?
What's the best way to get from here to the North side of town?
What are you going to be doing for the rest of the day?
How do you feel about the current state of the world?
How did you do on your test at school yesterday?
How do you deal with this summer heat?
How did you go about starting your own business?

Do you see the pattern here? All these questions begin with the words "what" or "how".

There are eight basic ways to begin questions: Who, What, When, Where, Why, How, So and Are. The easiest way to ask an open-ended question is with "What" and "How" but you can form an open-ended question with any of the eight.

If the question is structured correctly, it will force the person to open up and reveal information. Let's look at this in a business perspective. Going back to example in the previous Principle with Michael the Hustler and a mystery person, let's see how Michael completely opens up a potential prospect. The shop is set-up and the Tee's are on display. Instead of waiting for customers, Michael goes out to make one (creating, not waiting).

Michael: Hello. How's it going today? (Closed-ended question. Necessary to make sure the person is responsive)

Person: Fine, I guess.

Michael: Can I ask you a question real fast? (Closed-ended question. Used to "break the ice")

Person: Sure go ahead.

Michael: You're dressed very fancy to be on this side of town (Comment about the person – this starts the conversation). What are you doing out and about over here? (Open-ended question. Trying to get the person to open up and reveal information)

Person: Oh (smiling), I just came from a meeting. Now that I think about it, that's really the only time I come to this side of town.

Michael: Welcome back then, and by the way, you look like you're burning up in those clothes (smiles). (Comment about the person)

NOTE: Michael also could have asked an open-ended question here that relates to the information he just received about the person coming from a meeting such as, "What kind of business are you in?" or "What do you do for a living?"

Person: It is hot out here.

Michael: Hot? That's an understatement! I've been out here for hours (comment about himself). But I guess I have to deal with it; I need to move these T-shirts (Comment about himself). What do you think about them? (Open-ended question)

Person: They're nice. I like the colors you have.

Michael: These are in style right now. Matter of fact come and take a look, it doesn't cost anything to look. I won't keep you too long; you might pass out from the heat (laughs). (Comment about the situation)

Person: (Looks at the shirts) You know what? These are really nice, how much are they? (This person has just made a **SOI**. Michael would then proceed to qualify him or her. This is necessary to make sure that they have the ability to make a purchase, or future purchase, and they aren't just playing nice).

See how it all comes together? It takes a little practice but it's really very easy. Of course this is just the basics, but like I said, it will get you going in the right direction.

SIDE NOTE: If you would like to explore the techniques and power of conversation further please read, Holding Magnetic Conversations, written by yours truly. It's a summary of all the conversation techniques I've learned throughout the years. This short and easy to follow book is filled with real world proven techniques for talking to anyone, anytime, anywhere. It will teach you how to build rapport in a few seconds and pull them into your very own flame. All this is the very foundation to having a magnetic personality.

Principle 4: Question Techniques That Get Results

Here's something that may shock you. During the actual sale itself (not before or after the sale's process), you will only need to talk 30% to 40% of the time. The reason for this is because you'll be asking questions and letting the potential customer do the talking.

By asking the right questions, you lead the sale. You pull them along, not push them along. Your ultimate goal of course is to get the sale and unless the customer is extremely hungry for what you have, you will need to lead them all the way until that happens. We will talk about pushing later if it's necessary, but for right now absorb these techniques.

(1) **Return to Sender** – By far the easiest to work into a conversation. When a mail carrier delivers a piece of mail to a house where no one lives anymore, what does he or she do? They take it back to the mail facility so it can be returned to the sender. This is the same idea here. When a customer asks you a question, you return it with another question to make sure you are extracting the correct meaning. What better ways to know what customers want then to have them tell you! Let's get into an example with Michael.

Customer: So what kind of T-shirts do you have?

Michael: What kind of T-shirts are you looking for? Solid or something with a print on it?

Did you catch that? See how Michael returned the question with another question to get more information so he will know exactly what the customer wants? Let's look at it one more time.

Customer: What sizes do your shirts come in?

Michael: What size were you looking for?

If someone asks when you can come back, you return that question and ask them, "When is the best time for me to come back?" If someone asks you if you deliver, you return that question and ask them, "Would a delivery option help you the most?"

What you're doing here is leading your customer to the sale. If you can find out what they want and be able to give it to them, how can they say no to making the purchase?

There's a huge side benefit when you use this technique, it keeps you from assuming things. Let's say a customer asks Michael if he carried any older style Tee's. Instead of saying yes or no, Michael would ask, "Are you looking for some older styles?" Most people would automatically assume since the person asked about older styles, that they **were** looking for older styles. But what if the answer to Michael's question was, "No! I only want the **newest** styles."

Michael could have completely turned this customer off if he assumed and went into trying to sell him older styles. A missed opportunity due to lack of skill. Assuming is not your job. Your job is to give people what they want.

(2) **The Cross** – This technique takes a little more tact to work into a sales situation, but it is very powerful and worth the effort. What you're doing here is giving the person options. To keep things simple we'll make it just two or three options. With this technique you take the position that the sale has already been made. On to the example:

Customer: Ok, I like the blue with the nice print but I also like the orange one (ponders on their decision).

Michael: So which one should I bag up for you? The blue, the orange or both? (smiles)

Did you catch that? One more example:

Customer: Wow, I really like this shirt. Erg (frustrated), but I like this other one too. I just don't have enough for both. (Michael lets the silence go on for a few seconds, remembering to talk only 30%-40% of the time) Hmm… maybe I should just hold off.

Michael: Well maybe I can help you. I see you around here a lot I know I can trust you. Tell you what; you can get both shirts right now for fifteen dollars. If you can't do fifteen dollars I will take ten dollars now, but you'll owe me ten dollars later. So which works better for you?

In both these examples Michael gave options, but as he did this he also took the position that the sale had already been made. Let me explain.

In both examples above Michael never asked if they were going to buy anything. All he did was give them the option of which Tees they wanted or, in the second example, how they were going to pay.

To really drive home how effective this technique is, let's apply it to real life.

Let's say you're at home with your special someone and you think it would be nice to go out to eat. Instead of asking, "Hey, would you like to go out to eat?" take the position that both of you are already going out to eat. Just give them the option where you should go. Cross them up with, "So are we eating at an Italian or Mexican restaurant tonight?"

In sales, just as in life, you want to lead as much as possible. This technique works tremendously well in that department.

(3) **Pinning** (AKA the Tie-Down) – A successful sale is often a whole bunch of little parts added up to create a bigger part; similar to putting a puzzle together.

The puzzle pieces we are dealing with here are agreements. Little yeses that lead to the big final yes where everything is put together nicely and adds up.

Allow me to ask you a question. How would you like to be a multi-millionaire? If you were not already a multi-millionaire, you would most likely respond in one big yes. But why do you want to be a multi-millionaire?

Would you love the freedom to buy what you want? That would be great, wouldn't it? How about having time to really spend the way you want. Travel and see the world that would be fantastic, don't you agree? You would also have to agree with me that you could truly help your family and loved ones in a much larger capacity than you can now. In fact, if you played your cards right, you and your children would never have to work for anyone again. How can you not love that, am I right?

The above questions I just asked you all sold you on the idea of being a multi-millionaire. If you ever had just the smallest desire to become one, you probably answered yes to every question I just asked. Each question pinned you. If you really have the desire in you, you can't say no. Saying no would go against the whole idea of becoming a multi-millionaire. And wouldn't that be backwards?

Pins (or Tie-Downs) are questions that are structured in such a way that they illicit agreement from someone. If you have truly identified their problem and know you can solve it, they need to believe that as well. How do you get them to believe and agree? Well, you let them say yes. When you say it, it doesn't mean much. When they say it, it means everything.

Pinning questions can end with:

Wouldn't it?
Doesn't it?
Shouldn't it?
Couldn't it?
Won't it?
Can't you?
Don't you agree?
Am I right?
Don't we?

After reading that list, you can see how Pinning is extremely easy to work into conversations, can't you? Because it really isn't that complicated, don't you agree? And the simpler things are the easier they are to memorize, am I right? When things are easy to memorize that means they should be easier to use, shouldn't they? And any knowledge that is overly complex could sometimes become useless, couldn't it?

Learn to Pin. Small yeses, will eventually lead to the big final yes. And that's what we all want in the end, don't we?

These questioning techniques will save you not only valuable time, but also keep you in control of the sales situation.

CHAPTER 8

Down to Business – What Lies Beneath

If you've read this far then I congratulate you! Most people who buy books never read them or never get past the first three or so chapters. From the time you read the Forward all the way up to the three tools we have just covered, I have been purposely leaving out important information. Everything you learned up to this point has prepared you for the next few chapters.

Everything we've gone over so far is nothing but the foundation of our house. If the foundation is strong the house we build on top of it will be stable.

This is a book about business but so far we have talked very little about it. The reason is because there are so many books on the subject and most of them do not teach what skill-sets you need to know *before* you ever start. They go on and on but if the reader doesn't see himself or herself within the information then they won't use it. They won't know how to use it! Simple.

By now you should have a clear understanding that the basics of business are not complicated. All it takes is a little determination, the ability to step out of your comfort zone and a little know-how. What we've covered so far is the "What" and "Why". Now it's time to move on to the "How".

Like I told you, what I know works. It works because it's simple. It's been stripped of all its fluff and over-complication. As you continue through this book don't reject any of the ideas because they seem too simple. And at the same time, try not to make them anymore complicated then they are.

Now that we have a solid foundation for your success in business, the rest will be easy. It's now just a matter of doing the physical things necessary to get your business running at full speed.

In the chapters that follow I will be "rapid firing" concepts and ideas to you in what may appear to be no particular order. The reason for this is to keep your mind working. Your mind remembers information much better when it is actively working. This isn't a college text book. I'm not going to bore you with 30 page chapters on one concept or strategy. I'm going to give you just the basics. Just enough to get the wheels of your mind spinning and let it figure out how to best apply this knowledge to your situation.

As your mind works this way, you will remember a lot more of what I'm teaching, and that's what we want. I'm not here to hold your hand, I'm here to point you in the right direction and let you discover your own way. If I held your hand I would be depriving you of that feeling and sense of accomplishment that comes with success.

Please don't misread me; I'm not watering anything down. But I am leaving room for you to put the big picture together on your own. The more you practice these techniques and use them, the sooner they will become your own.

What good is a manual or book if it didn't let you get involved? Even novels get you involved. You care about the characters and what happens to them. For some reason business books and materials don't do this. They just spit out overly complicated information and expect you to get it all. And in the end you still don't understand what your first step should be. There just seems like there is just more to know. Am I right?

Well don't worry, everything I'm about to share with you is tested and proven to work in the real world. I use these techniques everyday in my business and I learned them from people who used them everyday in theirs. If they didn't get results then all of us would have failed. All these techniques are easy to use and easy to understand. They also don't take much money and because of that, you lower your risk factor.

Ok, enough with the lecture let's get into it. Over the next few chapters we will cover tactics, strategies and marketing, and then I can give you the final key that will unlock the essence of business and put everything together for you? Are you ready? Let's go!

"Don't do something until you can get it right, do it until you can't get it wrong"
- Geno Auriemma, college basketball coach

CHAPTER 9
Insider Tactics and Strategies

A Business from Nothing (Working "The Flip")

If you are bootstrapping your business then this technique you will love. If you are willing to start small you may never need a bank loan of any kind (although you may want to check into government grants). Hustler's Math is simply the process of dividing up your money for the sole purpose of growing (or starting) your business. Here's how it works.

Take 10% to 20% (no less than 10%) of your net (cash in pocket) income and save it. Put it up and don't touch it! This is the money you are going to "flip" (make grow). Remember when we talked about having a quota in Chapter Five of this manual (Principle Six)? Pull out those numbers that you have written down now.

Your first goal is to net **twice** as much as you do now. If you work a job, then this can seem unrealistic so this is where the math comes in. Even when you are running your business and it's turning a profit still put up that 10% to 20%.

So what do we do with this money? We flip it. We use it to invest either in starting our business from nothing or directly into the business we already have so it can grow.

Now, when do we do that? When you have enough money saved up to do everything you need to do with it. If you're starting a business on a shoestring budget (which usually means working out of your home) then make sure you have enough to cover the things you need, business license and other legal formalities, business cards, computer, etc. If you already have a business then save up enough to where you can either add to you inventory or maybe add another line of products to what you already offer (be careful here though, we'll talk about this more in the marketing chapter). Maybe you just want to improve on what you're already doing. Or perhaps you want to open up your first official location or a new location.

Word of caution here: Don't wait until everything is perfect! Things will **never** be perfect. If you have enough money saved to get your business cards. Go get them NOW. Have enough saved to get your business license? Don't wait, get it NOW. Haven't found that perfect storefront location? Who cares, if you have the products ready to go, start getting business NOW! Work with what you have now and fill in the blanks later. If you wait too long, that money you saved may just find someplace else to go. I hope you understand what I'm saying here.

Regardless of whether you are starting a business or already have one your eventual goal is to move up the Infamous Money Chain. And this is where you get the money to do that, without a loan or investors. It's not always possible, depending on your type of business, to go without a loan or investor's money but if you can do it then do it! In fact, if you get the ball rolling, potential investors will see just how serious and committed you are. Either way, you win.

That 10% to 20% you save is used strictly to make you more money. You'll be flipping it so that it can grow.

Best part about all this is the fact that even if you lose the money and things don't go as planned; it won't affect your lifestyle or your business. Again, little risk with a big potential for pay off. If possible, never spend money you don't have. Don't forget that bad financial decisions and record-keeping are the number one and number two killers of new businesses.

Let's look at our how "direct flipping" works. There is also compound flipping but that is a subject for another time.

If we take just two dollars and flip it just 20 times, we will be millionaires. Remember, flipping just means to double

$2
$4
$8
$16
$32
$64
$128
$256
$512
$1,024
$2,048
$4,096
$8,192
$16,384
$32,768

$65,536
$131,072
$262,144
$524,288
$1,048,576

Now, how do you like that math?

You want to double every dollar you invest. For my business educated readers that means a 100% ROI. To break that down it would mean you need to double your money. Turn one dollar into two dollars; turn three-hundred dollars into six-hundred dollars. Do you follow me? Is this model realistic? If you are starting from literally nothing, not entirely, but it gives us targets to aim for when we are ready to shoot.

Your money is not considered flipped until it has at least doubled. If you can triple it then do that! This is why our first goal is to double your net income; it will start you on the right road. In the mean time, if that means you have to live off of less money to put up that 10% to 20% then do it! The end rewards in the future are worth the sacrifice now.

Self branding – What do you represent?

What is in a brand? If you are not familiar with the word brand I will give you the dictionary definition.

Noun:
    A type of product manufactured by a particular company under a particular name.
Verb:
    Assign a brand name to.

These definitions are a little behind the times, but you get the general idea. In the modern business world a brand is not just a product that is manufactured or a product that holds a company's name. It is what the company itself represents, and with small business this means its owner as well.

When you begin a small business it is just you and perhaps a partner or two. And that is it. You must brand yourself. Your company and the company's product and service must reflect you. When your business grows it will take on a life of its own, but when you are "down and dirty" in those initial years, people are going to be looking at you and only you.

So, what do you represent?

Quality? Integrity? Personalized attention? Education? Only you can answer this question. Your brand must reflect both the market and/or industry you are in, and what product, service or idea you are bringing to the market. When you know what you represent, you can make sound business decisions, because everything must reflect you. If you represent integrity and you are a mobile car mechanic, then anything that may compromise that integrity doesn't need to be included in your thought process.

If you are a financial educator and write books and do seminars then at all times you must represent education. You don't write romance novels and you don't do seminars on how to make award winning Chili. There are exceptions of course, but when you break your brand (or confuse it), you are in violation of the Game – you are threatening the survival of your own business.

Proper branding whether personal (you) or business (company) or product, should accomplish three crucial things:

(1) Give a clear message about what you and/or your company represents in the market.
(2) Build customer loyalty by establish you and/or your company as the expert that can solve their problems.
(3) Connect to and motive the consumer. An emotional connection mixed with logic is best.

Remember this – as a small business, brand yourself *first*. Brand your business *second*.

When I mention Donald Trump what does he represent to you? Wealth, business, real-estate? And if I mention Oprah Winfrey? Wealth, business, media mogul? And how about Bill Gates? Wealth, business, technology?

Each of these individuals started with very few resources (excluding Trump) and became household names. How? By first branding themselves, doing what they represented and innovating in their particular field and industry.

When you think of their companies, you think of them as well. They are the face of their companies – The ultimate form of branding.

What face do you envision when I say McDonalds? You don't think of its founder Ray Croc, or the current CEO. You think of Ronald McDonald. Ronald is the face and representation of the company. A mascot is no longer a strong form of branding, although during the time period the company was formed and grew, it was. In this day and time, you are your small business mascot, so to speak.

Since the rise of social media, things are a lot more personal now. People want to know who they are dealing with, who is responsible and what they represent. Before you can answer these questions for others, you must first know the answers for yourself. To make your mark in the Game, you must brand yourself. Knowing what your represent is the first step, get on that right NOW.

Your Business Card and its Hidden Power

This is the most basic and overlooked tool in your business arsenal.

Everyone in business has one but almost no one uses this tool to its fullest potential. How many business cards have lost or misplaced? How many business cards do you just throw away? Unless you're in the highest levels of business, you really don't make it a point to keep and file away business cards. Why? Because they have no immediate value to you unless you need that product or service now, or in the near future. Add that to the fact they're just plain boring.

So how do we make your business card not only stand out but also have it do what it was designed to do (get you more business)? Good question.

The business card is the most overlooked form of advertising. If you're on a serious budget and you can't manage a full blown advertising campaign, you need to get creative. That little piece of stiff paper needs to have its own value. Let's look at a typical business card format.

You have the Company Name, some contact numbers (office, cell, fax, etc.), a website address, an e-mail address, the company address, business hours and the name of the contact person along with their title. Social Media information is also included. Sometimes the card may include a nice little company logo and a catchy slogan or description of what that person (or business) does. Standard stuff and rather plain.

Here's the Hustler's way. We include only the basics on our business cards.

- Our name (sometimes the title also)

- One or two contact numbers (probably business phone and fax. Or cell phone and fax. Or business and cell phone)

- The company name

- Website address

- E-Mail address

- Social Media information

And that's about it. I know what you're thinking. What I just described sounds extra dull and boring. But put your mind at rest, we need the extra room on our cards for some advertising space.

There are two things to do with this extra space:

(1) Turn your business card into a coupon. Think of it like a miniature flyer.

Imagine receiving a business card that actually allowed you to receive a discount on your purchase.

Intrigued? Now, this discount doesn't have to be a lot, maybe 10 or 15 percent. Would this get your attention? Of course it would. And it would get the attention of potential clients or customers too.

How about advertising an offer that allows a person a discount when they call in with an order? Or if they order on your website they get the discount. This is an interesting tactic because it drives website hits. Let your mind work out the details.

Now, does this "coupon" have an expiration date? No it doesn't. But you will need to track which of your customers has already cashed in their discount. More work in the short-term for more reward over the long-term.

This subtle form of advertising is very powerful and it's great for extra word of mouth business (the best kind of advertising). The person you give the card to gets a discount, and you can bet that if your product or service is top notch they will tell someone about you and they'll mention the discount. And when that referred person calls to get their discount, give it to them! It's not about if they have the card or not, it's about being consistent and being a man or woman of your word.

That leads me to mention this. Although your card is a coupon, you don't take it. Let your customer keep it, it is after all a business card. All that is required of them is to mention the discount. Now a word of caution here, do not give a discount that you cannot afford to give! Common sense but I need to make that clear.

What you're doing is giving value up front. That card becomes valuable because it solves a problem by itself. It's saving your customer money and allows them to "test you out" with slightly less risk to them. Are you with me on this? Giving value up front in this way will make an impression. It says, "Just give me a chance to impress you. And I know I will so I'm not worried about the few dollars I'm losing right now."

Last thing. This will not work in all businesses, please use your common sense to determine if this approach is right for you.

(2) Turn your business card into a membership card

Have you ever been to Sam's Club or to any of those membership clubs? They give pretty good value for the money and it just makes you feel special that you have the privilege to shop there. You can do the same thing here.

Anyone who holds your business card can come by your business location and get a special stamp on it. This stamp means they are now a member of your business. This means they can officially receive discounts on all purchases for a year, for three months, for any purchases over one-hundred dollars or whatever.

Again this is powerful and it's so easy to do. If you're creative enough, you can work things like this out even with online businesses or a Network Marketing business if it is allowed.

A few more points about the above methods. Business cards only have limited room so make the message stand out and be very clear. Something like this:

- Customers get 10% off with this card

- Bring this card & join now! Discounts on $100 or more

- Join our Elite Club and get 15% off!

When you write these small lines, make sure they're specific and they tell the people *exactly* what they're going to get. Something like: Special discounts – Call now! Is not going to cut it. And also, if possible, make sure these lines are bold and stand out, preferably near the center of the card.

The point here is to make your customer feel as though they're part of a special or private club. It's subtle but powerful if they feel they are getting a good deal.

Ok, one last thing. Don't be stingy with your business cards. They are your form of advertising until you can afford all those nice television and radio spots, so get them out there! If you go to a restaurant, leave one with your tip money. Did you just have your car serviced? Leave one with the person who helped you. Go to grocery stores and if they have a bulletin board, post a few up. Leave some in friendly businesses on their counters or bulletin boards. Since your card isn't just a card, it gives people a reason to actually take them; and more importantly **use** them.

Which One Are You?

There are three basic types of Hustlers. As you get out there and talk to people you're going to eventually run across fellow business owners. Some you want to network with, others you just want to avoid. Let's cover each briefly and talk about where you should be in this group.

(1) The first type is the lazy or part-timey Hustler. They make just enough money to get by. They are usually broke and stay that way because they lack the inner drive and motivation it takes to succeed. They're really not cut out for business and are better at playing employee. Sad to say, but sometimes they're too lazy to even keep one of those.

These part-timey Hustlers that do keep a job and hustle on the side are not true entrepreneurs. To really be an entrepreneur you have to experience business without a security net. That means you get no paycheck. You only make money off of the work you put into your enterprise. If you don't work hard and Grind (give your all to your business), you don't make money. Simple.

Don't misread me, if you have a job and use that money to get your business up and running that's well and good. But if you can't let that false sense of security go when it is time, you probably never will. And these people usually don't. You want to network with these Hustler's but realize their level of drive and commitment does not equal yours.

(2) The second type of Hustler is the backwards Hustler. He or she is similar to the lazy entrepreneur but the difference is they actually make money. They are just foolish with it and end up spending it all. We call them "backwards" because instead of keeping money and setting up situations where it can grow, they spend it foolishly and stay at the same place in their financial life. Or even worse, go backwards into a situation where they are constantly Grinding just to keep from going broke. Easy come, easy go as it's written. These are the Hustler's you want to avoid. They are not playing the Game properly.

(3) The last is the forward Hustler. They have made a mental transition when it comes to money. They know the hidden value of it. They use all their tools and knowledge to get ahead and move forward. And isn't that the point of business, to move forward? It's not to stand still and just survive and definitely not to put yourself in a worse position. If you want to Grind just to maintain, you can do that at a regular job with a hustle on the side. You want to network with forward Hustler's.

Bottom line, if you're not in business to make your life better and to help fulfill your goals and dreams you more than likely won't make it. It is too easy to throw in the towel when things get too hard. Make a firm decision and commitment to yourself now which side of the fence you want to be on.

Value each dollar you make and give gratitude for it. As an entrepreneur you have become (or will become) part of what makes this entire society work and function. That's not an easy weight to carry but it's definitely something to be proud of.

Know Your Customers and Know Your Product, Service or Idea

Enough can't be said about the businessperson who ignores or forgets one of the single biggest principles. You will not get as many sales as you want if you do not know your customer. And you cannot get those customers if you don't know your product (or service or idea).

So you think you have a good product or service and you feel it might change the world, or at least change *your* world when the money starts rolling in. But if you do not first check out and test the market you plan on selling to, you may never get your business off the ground. It's like playing darts in a pitch black room. Yes you're throwing the darts, but you can't see your target so you don't know where that darts are going.

What makes a product, service or idea great? As you should know by now, the way it solves people's problems. But are the masses looking for your particular product, service or idea? Are you trying to help solve a problem that people either don't have or aren't willing to pay for? It doesn't matter how great you think something is, what matters is how great the market and the masses think it is. They are the judge and jury, and they are the final word. The money they spend is the greatest testament to what they think is important or needed.

So if you are just starting out, or haven't begun yet, you must sit down and think a moment. Get a piece of paper and something to write with. What you need to do is to go over the benefits of your product, service or idea.

What do I mean by benefits? Quite simply the advantages or help your product or service will provide the customer. Let's look at a popular selling item that will never go away such as an automobile. Why do people buy cars? To answer that just look at the benefits:

- Freedom of movement. People can go anywhere anytime they choose.

- Self reliance. People do not have to depend on others to get around or wait on public transportation.

- With a vehicle you can transport and move things around; whether it's your family, friends, or packages, household items, etc.

- Saving time. You can get a lot more done in a day when you have transportation then you can without it.

But you know what the biggest benefit is when people go to purchase an automobile? Prestige. If they have the money people will spend big dollars just to ride around or be seen in a popular or stylish ride. It just so happens that a vehicle caters to some of the most important attributes buyers look for when they go to buy anything.

As you write down the benefits of your product, service or idea you must measure how they stack up to what's considered the basic desires of almost all human beings. Basic desires and the actual motivation to make a purchase are different, but do share similarities. We will cover purchase motivations in depth later in this book. For now here are ten basic human desires. People want to:

(1) Be Accepted. They desire to be liked and respected by others.

(2) Be able to save money and/or make more money as well as save time.

(3) Feel romance. People want to feel love from sources other than family and friends.

(4) Be respected for their ideals. This is a form of admiration. People with strong ideals want those ideals to be heard and respected. This is especially true in their circle of family and friends.

(5) Have social contact. Most people have a deep seated fear of being alone.

(6) Have status. Yet another form of admiration, people desire to reach the heights of their own social group. These heights of status are dictated largely by their current environment.

(7) To feel secure and at peace. These words mean different things to different people but every person desires a feeling of security in their environment.

(8) Be able to determine their own fate. People desire to feel in control of their own lives as well as having the freedom to make their own choices.

(9) Eat. Getting food and water are the most basic survival instincts we have.

(10) Wield influence and power. No matter how buried this desire is, human beings want to be influential to others. Influence is a prerequisite to power.

There is a much deeper level to these desires but now I want you to realize, every coin has two-sides. So the 10 desires I've just listed for you have opposites. What I'm about to tell you is very important.

Everybody wants (desires) something, and everyone fears something. For those 10 items above, every person has a fear, however slight, that one of those desires will not be fulfilled. Said another way, people want pleasure and want to avoid pain. It's basic human nature and it's simple.

Let's look at number two on the list. If people want to save time, they will never spend money on things they feel will waste their time. Do you follow me? If you don't, then you need to ask yourself why fast food restaurants are so popular.

So what's the point of all this? You must make sure your product, service or idea is desirable to the people you want to sell it to. It must give the people at least one benefit from that list of basic desires. The ideal situation would be two or more benefits from the list. If your product, service or idea does not, you may need to either re-think your product or service line, or learn to make your product or service cater to these basic desires. This simple trick has a lot to do with marketing which we'll discuss in greater detail in the marketing chapter.

When you know your customer, you will know what they want. If you can get them what they want and do it with good quality and at a good price, you will make money. Know who you're trying to sell to first, then go get (or create) something to sell them.

Final Note: You must make an effort to learn everything about your product, service or idea. Know it up, down, backwards, forwards, in and out. When you know your customer and you know your product in this way, you cannot only give them a long list of benefits, but you can also educate them in the process. Sometimes people have problems they didn't even know they had. Get my drift?

The Bird Dog (Generating Word of Mouth Advertising)

Marketing is a funny thing. People are less likely to accept what you have to say about your business then what someone else has to say about your business. It's because of this principle of the human mind that word of mouth advertising has always, and will continue to be, the best advertising. I mean whose opinion would you trust more? Your best friend's opinion or someone who you don't know?

Many big companies make a huge mistake here because they don't have a "face" so to speak. They just have a name. Don't get me wrong, names are very powerful but only after you either experience it yourself, or someone you know and trust tells you about it.

If you're shoe stinging your business you must rely almost completely on word of mouth to get you customers. There's no way around it. You must start the ball rolling, and let your new customers help push it along until it builds its own momentum.

Now you can pray this happens or you can make it happen. Remember, Hustlers create, not wait. So now I will share with you how to generate powerful advertising for yourself without the big budget.

"With marketing, invest in people first. Invest with the media later."
- W. James Dennis

Your business is all about people. I don't care what you're selling; the end result is that someone has to pay for it. Network Marketing has already figured out how powerful word of mouth is. Instead of spending big money on radio and television campaigns, they rely on people. And people get paid just for doing what they do anyway; recommend things they like to the people in their life.

If you're already in a Network Marketing company then fantastic, but if not, you need to take this strategy and apply it to your business.

The highest form of customer service is making the customer feel valued and appreciated. Not like they're a pain in the ass. Have you ever experienced bad customer service? Of course you have. How did it make you feel? Like the company could care less and just wanted your money? Would you recommend that company to your family or a friend? More than likely not; and neither would anyone else. Word of mouth whether bad, or not given at all will kill your business. And it's a slow painful death, trust me.

Since making your customers feel valued and appreciated is the best road to travel on, then how do you do this? Well this method involves a little bit of sacrifice up front, but the end rewards you receive are well worth it.

Remember when we talked about using the power of your business card? Well that gets people through the door. Now that they're in your world, this is your time to make an impression. In other words, give them a reason to come back. This means you should be giving your all to your customers. Make no exceptions when it comes to being there for them. Handle complaints and give them the best service you possibly can (and a fair price too).

Now if you've done your job correctly they will come back. If a customer comes back, you've got them. You have brought them into your world. Now since they obviously like what you do and how you do it, what can we do to not only keep them but to influence them to bring a friend? This strategy is called the bird dog.

In real life, the bird dog is an actual dog that fetches the ducks and geese that a hunter has shot down. In business, a bird dog is a satisfied customer who is rewarded for bringing you more customers.

When a customer comes back to you (or depending on your type of business – the first time they come to you), you must have a system in place that can reward them for bringing you another customer. You can offer them a discount on their next purchase when they bring a friend, a special membership which may include special pricing, free samples, the opportunity to get the new products before everyone else, etc. If you think about it you can come up with something. The Big Boys do this in various forms all the time.

Now what does this do? It makes the customer feel valued and appreciated. What did you lose in the process? You may be thinking money but let's look at something real fast.

Michael the Hustler gets a new customer. Let's call her Jessica. Jessica comes to buy four shirts from Michael. Michael gives a special discount for first time customers. Buy four items get one free. So for forty dollars, Jessica has gotten four shirts and a sports hat. Five items in all (she decided she didn't need a fifth shirt).

Seasons change and new styles are released. It just so happens Jessica comes back to Michael to purchase these new styles. Michael explains to her, that he will give her any shirt or sports cap she wants for only seven dollars in the future for every customer she brings him. The new customer she brings will of course get the buy four get one free deal and Jessica's next shirt or cap will be 30% off. Not a bad deal for someone who buys a lot of shirts or sports caps.

Jessica loves the shirts and sports caps and likes Michael as a person. She has no problem telling her best friends about this guy she knows that has these really good shirts for cheap.

Now here's the math. That one customer just brought Michael over eighty dollars. That's just upfront. Now Jessica's friend will bring another person, then they will bring another person and so on and so on. Michael lost a little profit up front, but in the long run he sold more products with less work and has gained the most important thing – long-term regular cash flow.

Understand Game – **Your customer's value isn't what they spend with you today, but what they spend with you over the years they do business with you.**

The main goal of every business is to get customers and keep them! You keep customers by treating them well and letting them reap the rewards of sharing with their friends and family.

This, my friend, is yet another reason it's so important to start your business with money put aside to take care of your basic needs. It's slow at first, but the word of mouth will have people knocking down your door in the end. And the best part in all of this? Michael didn't do any extra work to get these new customers! The money he may have spent on advertising (other than business cards and flyers) was given to his customers as a, "Thank You". Matter of fact, in the long run, it was much cheaper.

Of course to continue to grow his business, Michael would have to get into traditional forms of advertising such as radio, television, online, etc. But in the beginning stages, Michael spent less money and had a lot less risk.

All Profit Is Made the Day You Buy Something

This is a simple concept to understand. If you sell anything that requires you to purchase something first, then you need to make sure you get that product (or components of a product) at the best possible price you can find.

The cheaper you can get your products or the equipment you use to provide your service, the more profit you will see in the long run.

Find the best wholesaler or place to purchase those things. Now just because you have the ability to get what you need for cheaper doesn't necessarily mean you drop your price to your customer. This does however make it easier to offer those discounts and bird dog programs we have talked about.

As the saying goes, buy low and sell high. Remember we are trying to direct flip our money. Meaning we want to get as close to a 100% return (doubling our money) on what we spend as possible.

Another reason we buy low is because if worse comes to worse, you should be able to at least sell your stock at the price you paid for it to break even and get your money back.

Find the best quality at the best price. Then you can offer the best quality at a reasonable price. Over many years in business, you will appreciate those quarters and dollars you saved because it all adds to your bottom line; profit.

The Transaction (What's Involved in a Sale?)

A sale is nothing more than a series of steps. Each one takes over where the one before it leaves off. Follow the steps, get the results. No, you will not make every single sale, but your chances are better by following these guidelines. You know I'm all about simplicity so there are just five steps. After those steps we'll cover **qualifying** the prospect in detail.

(1) The Introduction – This is something you must *make* happen. This is the process where you let the potential customer know what you have available. Again, this can be done verbally or in writing (such as with a flyer passed out in your part of town). If people don't know what you're doing, you won't have any customers. So let people know what you do in the most effective way for your type of business.

(2) The Offer – When you find or hear from someone who gives a **SOI** (show of interest) then it's now your job to sell yourself first (which can be done in less than 30 seconds in person or over the phone). Once they are brought into your world, then move into what it is you sell (product) or do (service). Then you move into qualifying the potential customer to make sure they have a problem that you can solve.

A) They show a **SOI**
B) You sell yourself (bring them into your world)
C) Qualify them

(3) The Show And Prove – Once you have the customer looking through your inventory or at least asking a lot of questions, you have them in your

world! Now keep them there. If you've properly qualified them, now is the time to begin to use your mouthpiece. Ask questions; get them down to what it is they want exactly. During this process of showing, you may also need to prove to them the quality and value of what you have to offer. If you know your product, service and industry like you're supposed to, then it's simply a matter of educating your customer on why they should do business with you, the expert.

(4) The Close – This is you asking for the sale. Many people miss the sale because they never ask the simple question, "Is this the one you want?" or "I can do everything I promised, so when can we get started?" Remember you are leading at all times and the close is where you're leading them to. Some people need a little more of a push than others and this is where you may need to do it. Not before! This is also the best time to stop talking even more (we'll cover the close in more detail in our next section on The Push).

(5) Contact and/or Referral – Don't just let your customers go! Give them a reason to come back. Or let them go the first time and when they do come back give them a reason to bring a friend or family member next time. It is a good idea to get a phone number and/or possibly an e-mail address from all your customers. This makes it easy to keep them informed about changes to your service or product line. Also it's a nice way to let them know about special deals and discounts. If you cannot solicit them for this information, then send them away with a small flyer that explains your "bird dog" program. Just don't call it a bird dog program. You get my point – work smarter, not harder. Let one successful sale lead you to others. You're not about just selling; you're trying to build a business too.

A Quick Note on Qualifying

We've talked a lot about this but it's so important that I wanted to cover it again. When you are qualifying you are making sure of three very important things:

(1) The person you are talking to is the person who can make the purchase. Don't waste time trying to sell to someone who isn't making the buying decision.

(2) Make sure the person you're talking to can buy right then and there. If they don't have the money then you can set up payment plans or let them go and tell them that if they come back they can get a first time buyer discount, etc. Again, don't waste time selling to people who can't hand over the cash.

This doesn't mean ignore their questions or be rude. What I'm saying is just give them enough information that they will want to come back and do business when they do have the money.

(3) Make sure your customer and your product or service match. If you can't solve their problem the way *they want* it solved and they refuse to listen to what you have to say on the topic, then let them go. Don't waste your time. But for extra effect (and to keep a good reputation), refer them to someone who *can* help them. This is an important point to build up your Network which we'll talk about later in this chapter. Refer business to fellow business owners and have them do the same for you.

The Push – Handling Objections to Get To the Close

It's going to happen sooner or later so I need to prepare you for it. During the closing part of the sales transaction, people are going to get cold-feet and stop the forward motion of the sale. Basically they are going to give reasons and excuses (objections) as to why they should not buy what you have to sell.

Your job, as always, is to lead them to the sale. But at this point you can't lead you have to push a little. You must get past all their excuses, doubts, fears, worries or whatever else they come up with and get to the real reason, the root of the objection.

Sad to say, most people's objections are not even realistic. They are just making things up to throw you off balance. Sometimes people are just asking you (in their own special way) to convince them even more why they should part with their money.

This is a real simple process and only requires that you know a few basic points (you knew a numbered list was coming, didn't you?):

(1) Remind them of the positive then keep asking questions to get to the root of their objection. When you can see the root of the weed, it is easier to pull the entire root out of the ground.

(2) Once you identify the root you must prove to them why their objection is not valid. Educate your customer. Not in a demeaning way, but in a way that establishes you as the expert.

(3) Once you have them in agreement (pinning them with the right questions is very effective here), then go for the close again.

These three steps are all based around your understanding of the "Why". If you can't answer "Why" the customer should buy, or "Why" they should choose you over your competition, then it will be very difficult to push the sale.

Let's visit Michael and see how this works. Michael has followed standard procedure. He's opened up the prospect, qualified them, shown and proved to them why his products and customer service are the best, but the prospect is still hesitant on handing over the money. Michael isn't turned off by this at all; he still goes toward the close but has to take a detour called pushing.

Now the customer hasn't left yet and is still looking around so they are obviously interested. So what's going on? Let's see how this plays out.

Michael: Since you're a first time customer I have the buy four get one free discount I can give you. So these five shirts will only be forty dollars.

Customer: Yes, I know but I usually get my shirts from the mall, I'm not sure about these.

Michael: Well I see. I've already told you about my refund and exchange policy and you have my business card. I've also shown you the quality of the shirts and I think we can agree that it's top notch (reminding the customer of the positives). There's no difference between my quality and mall quality except the price. Now, forty dollars for five shirts is a great deal, isn't it (pinning)? Should I bag them up or would you prefer them boxed? (Michael uses the cross question technique. A subtle way of pushing)

Customer: (Looking doubtful) Eh, no that's ok I think I'll just stick with the store I regularly go to. Thanks anyway.

Michael: Well before you go can I ask you something?

Customer: Sure I guess.

Michael: Well I've been having these shirts available (Michael doesn't use the word selling) for a long time and I can't see why anyone would pass up a deal like this. Did I do something wrong (asking a question to begin getting to the root of the objection)?

Customer: (Looking slightly confused) What? No, it's not you.

Michael: Well I don't want to make this mistake again in the future so could you tell me why you've decided against my offer (another question to get to the root of the objection)?

Customer: No, no. The shirts are great and it is a great deal but I feel more comfortable shopping where I normally shop. (Michael takes note of this statement. Could this possibly be the root? Michael decides to check to see if it's the price. Price is a very common objection)

Michael: Well fair enough. Just curious, how much would you pay for five shirts where you shop at? (Another question to see if this is the root of the objection)

Customer: Well, let's see. For five shirts like these, probably about eighty dollars. Unless I caught a sale.

Michael: (Realizing that he still has this customer in his world because he hasn't left) So you would rather spend eighty dollars instead of forty? I guess I did do something wrong (realizes that the price may not be the real objection so he must keep digging). So is this an issue of trust (another question, still digging for the root)?

Customer: Well, (thinks for a moment – Michael says nothing) I guess it is. I mean how do I know that you'll be around? What if my shirt fades when I wash it or it falls apart (the customer laughs and so does Michael)?

Bingo! We've found the real objections – Trust and a lack of confidence in quality.

Michael: Good question so let me ease your mind. You have all my contact information and if for any reason I can no longer be here I'm only a phone call or email away. I can meet you anywhere on this side of town, even at your job if you'd like. I actually do that for a lot of my customers. You say you have a problem and it's my job to solve it. Now what clothing store do you know that would actually make a delivery to your job?

(Now that Michael knows the real objection he proves why it's not valid by explaining why his customer service is better than that of a common retail store. He personally delivers his products, which means the customer saves time. He continues to push.)

Michael: And don't forget, you're saving forty dollars here and if they're crap Tee's, which they're not, what have you really lost (again reinforcing the positive)? So let me prove all this to you. I'll bag these up, you take them, try them out and if you're not happy I'll refund all of your money no questions asked. Now that's a rock solid guarantee, wouldn't you agree (pinning)?

(Michael goes directly for the close. He doesn't allow his customer to get a word in just yet.)

Customer: I dunno...

Michael: If these shirts are everything I say they are you'll be saving a lot of money in the future. Just give me a try (again a reminder of a positive and another subtle push).

Customer: What the hell. I'll give you shot. You seem like you're serious about your business.

Michael: If you only knew (makes a joke to relive some of the tension that has built up)!

The key to remember is that an objection is like an onion. It has layers. You just ask questions to pull away the layers and get to the core. This takes a little practice but once you have it down, you will raise your sales rate by about 20 - 40%. And that is a nice chunk of change in your pocket that could have gotten away in the long-term.

Network Marketing – The Good, The Bad and The Sacrifices

One of the most effective ideas of the last few decades is the concept of Multi-Level Marketing (MLM) also called Network Marketing. What makes this concept effective is the concept of leverage. As applied to Network Marketing, it is investing a little for a high return.

For a few hundred dollars or less you can plug yourself into a well oiled machine and reap the benefits of residual income. That is, income where you can constantly get paid for the work you've already done, plus you get paid on the work you're doing now and also other people's work. Ideally this situation can last you for a lifetime. It's a good deal. That's how music artists, actors, some authors, etc. get paid.

Residual income is another form of leverage. You spend a lot of time and put forth a lot of effort in the beginning, but the rewards in the end are well worth it. For a small monetary investment, you have the backing of thousands of people who can help you and educate you. You don't have this advantage as a solo-preneur. You can be taught to avoid many mistakes and pitfalls and if you're really serious, you can get on the ground and running in very little time.

If you're struggling to find an idea to begin a business with, Network Marketing could be your life raft in an ocean of uncertainty.

Unfortunately, like any business, some Network Marketing companies can end up unstable and fall apart within their first few years. Others are well established and will continue to be around for some time. Regardless of what the company is, they usually have a line of products and they tell you to use them, and find more people who are willing to do the same.

And this is where the problem lies – finding people, recruiting them, training them and keeping them. To truly be successful in Network Marketing, it is not so much about finding customers for the company's product or service; it is about bringing people into the program. If you thought selling was difficult, wait until you try relying on unreliable people. It can be very frustrating.

You must realize not everyone is entrepreneurial minded, and not all people make it a point to keep their word. You may find five people who say they will come sit at a presentation, and only one will show. And of those people that do finally invest, most will leave when they see they're not making money immediately. Many people expect something for nothing, and that is just not how business works. You can never let any of this stop you though, you must keep it moving like a true Hustler.

All in all, if you're not lazy and willing to put in the work, Network Marketing can be a very rewarding experience. So get on the internet and do some searches and see what you can find. Important note here: Find a company that sells things you, yourself, are interested and believe in. That commitment to the company's products in very important and makes your job a lot easier. Especially when you present these things to other people which is what Network Marketing is all about. You want to present with confidence, don't you?

One sacrifice that you will be making is you will be losing a level of freedom. Most Network Marketing companies have fairly strict guidelines on how you must present yourself and their products and/or service. They design everything, from business cards, to stationary, to promotional flyers, etc. This can strain your creative muscles. But again, this is part of the Game, and you must respect it. They want their business to survive, and as long as that business survives, you have the potential to make money as well. That's a fair exchange, isn't it?

All the principles, tools and most of the techniques in this book can be applied to beginning and growing a Network Marketing venture. Take the time and learn how to apply them, they will save you frustration and more importantly, time.

The Price Points Concept and Basic Negotiation

So what is a price point? To keep things simple, all it means is setting your product or service at the right price for the market you're trying to reach.

If you are selling disposable cigarette lighters like the kind you find at your local gas station, charging ten dollars for one is ridiculous. And if you did that I can assure you that you will never sell one unless someone is extremely desperate or just born yesterday.

Now on the other hand, if you sold high-end lighters that were made with stainless steel casing and could be refilled with butane and flint, charging ten dollars would be too low. Lighters like this can cost as much as a hundred dollars. Mainly because once they're bought, the customer won't need another one unless they lose it, or they collect them. A lighter of this quality can literally last a life time. If you could sell lighters like these at ten dollars you would make sales but very little profit. Not the ideal situation.

A proper price point is a tricky thing. Because of the way the human mind works, if something is priced too high, they may reject it. And if it's priced too low they will question the quality. Would you buy a new car tire from me for one dollar? No you wouldn't.

The consumer's mind is a fickle place. Huge companies spend millions per year trying to figure out the consumer, their buying patterns and trends. A creative company will create a desire, but when that desire fades, so do they. That's just the nature of fads; they come and go.

So when you begin to get your business up and running and you're trying to decide what you should charge for what you offer, there are a number of factors to consider:

(1) Nobody knows you. Surprise, surprise! You must create a means to get your share of the market with the bigger companies who are offering the same products and/or services you are. This almost automatically means that your prices must be similar if not lower than theirs. At the same time, your marketing costs will be fairly high as you get the word out about your business. Here's the rub on that. If you can make your product and service appear more valuable than theirs, you can get away with charging more. You can have what is called a niche product. A niche product is usually unique, one of a kind and marketed to a small group of passionate people. Think, commemorative collectable coins. It's all about perception and we'll talk about that in the marketing chapter.

(2) Remember when we covered the fact that all profit is made the day you buy something? Well this is another reason why. If you buy low, it's easier to sell low, *if* you have to.

(3) Location, location, location. How close is your business to other businesses similar to yours? And have you chosen an all around good location for your business? Some businesses don't need a physical location. Some can be mobile; others can be run completely over the internet. The fact remains however, you have to have somewhere people can go to (or get to) for a sense of legitimacy. Product or service quality, combined with customer service is more important than location in the long run but a good convenient location is an extremely valuable asset in the beginning.

(4) A proper budget for your business must be established. You need to know how much everything costs to run and maintain your business down to the penny. I'm not a big fan of paper work, but I'm a big fan of profit. If paper work helps me see more profit, I'm all for it.

(5) What are the others in your market or industry charging for similar products or services? You must do your research. The bulk of this research can be easily done online now. It's easy to do; it just takes an investment of time.

When you take all these factors into consideration you must come up with a fair price to charge people and still be able to maintain and grow your business. We are about growth here after all.

When businesses price products have you noticed how they use the less five cents or 99 cent structure? As in – $5.95 or $10.99 or $8.45. It was a common belief that people see these prices and think that they are less then what they really are. Now seriously, $10.99 *is* $11, who are we fooling? After tax, what are we saving? A couple of cents? But in the minds of the consumer they don't see $11 they see $10 plus some change.

This theory is slowly dissolving, it was a psychological trick but now we are beginning to see straight and rounded prices in the market like $12.50 or $25 for example. The modern consumer is smarter than you may know. Show them that respect at all times.

When price pointing, if you can charge just 5% - 10% less than the other people (if you have to), then you are on the right track.

If your business is based on the market, meaning your product is worth whatever people are willing to pay (such as online auctions, paintings, custom jewelry, etc), then you must be careful not to overcharge and still be fair to yourself. In demand public speakers for instance have been known to charge up to ten-thousand dollars or more for only a few hours of their time. Sounds outrageous? But in their line of work this is a very fair price. So know your market in and out and you will come up with the right price point in time.

Do not be afraid to experiment. You may not get it right the first time, but if you listen to your customers, they will steer you in the right direction. Just remember, be fair to your customers and allow enough profit for you to flip money so your business can grow. Do not violate the Game!

Now, another consideration in your final adjustment of price points lies in negotiating room. Negotiating room with your customers or clients is what we'll be talking about here. Standard business negotiation techniques we don't have room to cover but some of the principles are very similar.

As your business grows some of your regular customers and new customers are going to ask for you to come down on your prices. They are going to want a deal or a discount for themselves. It's going to happen, that's just how it is. Your average person wouldn't walk into a well known establishment such as a Target or Macy's and ask for a deal or a reduced price, but you're not a well known established company, so they are going to try you on this.

If you have the proper price point for your products or service, coming to an agreement that both people are happy about shouldn't be a problem. And that's the key here; both parties need to be happy with the deal. Regardless of how you weigh this, you are losing a little money upfront. Don't be discouraged! Remember; think of the long-term value of this customer. Instead of worrying about a loss upfront, think of all the profit over the length of their business with you.

A sale to a customer is just that, a sale. A returning customer is consistent revenue. More revenue means faster growth.

"A bird in hand, is worth two in the bush."
- Old European saying

A discount now with the potential for more purchases later, is much better than just one purchase now at full price.

An important point to keep in mind is to make sure you let this customer know that you are only doing this deal once. This is not and will never be a standard practice. Make sure they understand that so there is no confusion later.

You can always make up the difference on the next few sales so if you can work the deal you both agree on, then just do it! Don't squabble over only getting eight dollars when the regular price is nine dollars. Of course the more expensive your product or service, the bigger they will want the deal or discount to be so don't be too rigid about it, or too loose either. Again, only come down and work deals out if you can. I suggest that you do, but I'm not running your business.

If you are hard pressed to get the maximum profit out of every sale then let your customer know that, in a nice way of course. "Please don't tell me what I need to charge for my product (or service)," should get the point across pretty well.

Mental preparation is also important here. In your mind, you should have your figures worked out on deals and discounts, especially on multiple purchases at one time.

Using Michael as an example, his shirts go for ten dollars each. Although he doesn't say it, or even advertise it, he knows that he is willing to let three shirts go for twenty-five dollars. If that situation ever comes where he has to do that he'll simple act like it's a slight pain in the ass for him to do, and then do it anyway. He hasn't lost anything, and he was prepared for it.

Unless you're hard pressed for every penny I want you to look at it like this – would you rather have sold a few products or still have them sitting and collecting dust on the shelves? It's ok to bend sometimes, just don't break.

SIDE-NOTE: Here are two exceptions: If this customer is consistently bringing you new business or doing a lot of business with you, always discount their purchases. Or if this customer can offer discounts or freebies in their business, then do likewise. This is bartering, a win-win situation. Again, the long-term benefits outweigh the short-term gain.

Scouting & Opening up Territory (For the Brick & Mortar Start-up)

If you're on a tight budget (shoe stringing), and you are in the position where you have to get a physical location such as a store front or even a flea market (swap-meet) booth, here are some things to look for.

None of the knowledge contained in this book means anything if you need a place to sell and don't have one. So scouting out potential areas is a very important skill. Again, the right location in the start-up stages can make you or break you.

Location, location, location.

When you are scouting, the most important thing to remember is this. Are the people in that area even interested in what you are trying to sell or do? So, how do you find this out? You ask them. That's right! Take yourself into that area and ask the people who pass by if there was a store or a booth (or whatever) in this location would it be something that they would be interested in. Don't be shy about this; it's very necessary and harmless. Just introduce yourself as a business owner looking for a potential new location and people will respond. Also ask surrounding business owners, you'll find that most of them are very helpful with information. I said most, not all. This is also a great time to hand out those business cards.

While you're doing all this asking around, take products with you if you can. Let people see them. Be careful here because there are laws against this practice, but if you're not taking money then you've done nothing wrong (in most states and counties).

If you are offering a service then take flyers or brochures with you. It's never too early to start advertising. And who knows, you may just pick up a customer or two in the process. This is a great leverage of your time.

Here are some more things to look for when scouting:

(1) Foot traffic – You want to see a lot of people in the area, walking around and shopping.

(2) Other businesses in the area – This of course means more foot traffic and more potential customers! The owners, managers and employees are people too and may be interested in what you're selling.

(3) Test both "sides of the street" – This may sound strange to you, but you'll be amazed how business could be good on one side of the street and not on the other. Or better even just a few blocks away. Be thorough in your scouting and don't think one side of the street is a reflection of the area as a whole.

(4) Test your find – Even when you think you have a good location you want to look at it from different times of the day and different days of the week. How is the foot traffic in the morning, around lunch time, in the evening and at night? How is the traffic on the weekend compared to the weekday? Did you know Tuesday is generally the slowest retail business day of the week? And the first and last weeks of the month are usually the busiest? There are exceptions to this, but that's the general rule.

You will also be amazed at how the morning and afternoon can be slow and the night busy or vice versa. You will also find that people's attitudes differ from day time to night time. People in the day time are usually a little more uptight. They have schedules to keep and commitments on their mind. People are more relaxed in the evenings and at night.

Scouting takes time and patience, but discovering a good spot is well worth the effort. Also make sure that the price is right for your office space, retail space, booth, etc.

So once you've found a place, it's time to "open it up". That means beginning to generate traffic and customers.

Again, here are a few pointers to get you going in the right direction:

(1) Establish a regular schedule – This is a no-brainer. But depending on your business type you may need to adjust your hours of operation to serve as many people as possible. Remember when you were scouting and I told you to watch the foot traffic at different times of the day? Well this is why. Make your schedule revolve around the best flows of this traffic.

(2) Have the owners, managers and employees in the surrounding area (about a 10 to 15 mile radius if possible) know what you do. Just walk into an establishment, ask to speak with the owner or manager and hand them a business card. Tell them what you do, where you're located and take their business card as well. You never know, they may become customers or they may refer customers to you. And if you're speaking with one of your customers and they have a problem that one of your local business associates can solve, then refer them there. Also leave business cards, flyers and brochures in these establishments for their customers, if they allow you to. And take theirs and put them in your store. These are very important networking tools.

(3) Make yourself known – Don't just sit at your shop waiting on business, get up and stand in front of your store and meet people. Hand out business cards and flyers. Go to the closest gas stations and grocery stores and do the same thing after your business has closed for the day. The best time to do this is in the evening or at night when people are more receptive, but don't neglect the morning crowd. Remember, you don't have the money to fully advertise, but you do have the time. Use it wisely. Even if none of these people become customers, they will know you and what you do. Also they may just know someone who *does* need your product or service. People are a lot more comfortable dealing with people they know. So make yourself someone they know.

These are the basics. Again, simple but very effective. As you're opening up your territory make it a point to keep meeting people and sharing what you do with them for at least four to six months. At least three days a week if you can. Five days a week is even better. Whatever you do, don't get discouraged! All of this takes time and as long as you're putting in the effort it will come back to you. Just keeping pushing and sooner or later, you will see the results in your business.

Building a Customer Base and Keeping It (The Truth of Long-Term Value)

We've talked about this earlier but this principle is so important we need to discuss it in greater detail.

Learn to never look at your customer as just that one sale. That is not where their true value is. Those twenty dollars you get from them today, for example, should never be the judgment of how you treat them and the quality of service you provide. Just because they're spending twenty dollars and your average customer spends one-hundred, you need to treat them the same. That initial sell can turn into a lot more money over a length of time.

Big law offices are usually guilty of this type of behavior. They treat the clients with big money a lot better than the client with little money. But every business needs a steady cash flow to keep it operating, can we agree on that? This "little guy" that they just gave no regard to could have come back to them in the future; he could have referred one of his business associates or clients to them who *would* have paid the big dollars.

The point is – you never know who your customers are and who they know. This is the key to good customer service. And good customer service is the key to building and keeping a large customer base.

A solid customer base is like the roots of a great oak tree. You want them to run deep so that the tree itself remains strong against even the worst weather.

Consider this; it is a natural human response to care more about people who care about you. And also to give more interest to people who show interest in you.

Treat every customer just as important as the next. That small spender of twenty dollars could maybe spend thousands with you over the course of a year. Even if they, themselves, aren't the big spenders, they may refer people to you who are. But if this initial customer got crappy service, or a product, and was treated like they were unimportant, do you think they're coming back? More than likely not, and those future thousands of dollars will go to someone else.

It's not enough to just bring people into your world, you have to keep them there. And this is accomplished by the understanding that, over the long-term, you want those customers to spend a lot of money with you. Treat them well every time, put your best foot forward at all times and you will find that you will keep more customers. The side effect of this of course, is that you will also get more customers through word of mouth alone. A steady stream of revenue is the life blood of your business; make your job easier by not doing anything to cut off that supply. This is a very important aspect of the Game, play it properly.

Break Them Down With Association

Here's a very powerful principle, and one that is often overlooked. You will sooner or later run across a customer or client that is known and liked by a lot of people. If you're fortunate, you will run across a lot of these people.

Remember when we discussed the fact that people will believe what others say about you more than what you say about yourself? Well if you can't get a long list of testimonials from your satisfied customer base, you can still use their name. Not in an illegal fashion such as in writing or on advertisements, but you can mention this person during conversations with potential new clients and customers.

Dropping names correctly and at the right time can almost completely break down the wall of doubt people have about you and your business. When people find out that you associate with people they already know and trust they are more likely to trust you as well.

Let's see this strategy in action as Michael uses it. Before we begin let me set up the scenario for you. Michael is scouting out some new territory and making his way around to talk to business owners, managers and employees in the area. Mrs. Johnson is a fairly well known and respected business owner in the area and is a regular customer of Michael's.

Michael walks into a nearby office and introduces himself and asks to speak to the owner or manger. The manager comes out and Michael goes on to make his regular introduction:

Michael: Hello how are you doing today? My name is Michael and I am in the area just to hand out some flyers and business cards. I just wanted to leave some for you and your employees if that's acceptable. Can I ask your name?

Manager: Nice to meet you, my name is Jeff.

Michael: (Shaking hands) Nice to meet you too. I won't take up too much of your time I just wanted you and your employees to know what I do. I am the owner of, *Right Time T-Shirts and Lids*. I offer high quality T-shirt and sports caps for low prices in the area. Can I leave you with some flyers? There's a coupon on it that gives all first time buyers a discount just for trying me out.

Jeff: (Hesitant) Well, I guess so.

Michael: (Hands over some flyers to Jeff) If you could please put these somewhere where your employees can see them I would appreciate it. Or with your permission I can hand these out myself. (Before giving Jeff a chance to respond) By the way do you know Mrs. Johnson who owns the, *Tiny and Tidy Day Care* around the corner?

Jeff: Oh yes, Mrs. Johnson. A few of my employee's children go to that Day Care.

Michael: Oh really? She's such a sweet lady. We talk all the time, have you ever met her?

Jeff: Sure a few times, she does seem pretty nice. She's had the Day Care up there for about 10 years I was told.

Michael: That's what she told me. I hope to be in business that long myself! We'll see how it goes (laughs). Anyhow, she's a really good customer of mine so some of your employees would probably like to get some quality T-Shirts and sport caps like she does.

Jeff: (An obvious change of attitude) Well, I guess so. So what kind of T-shirts do you carry and how much are they (Jeff gives a **SOI**)?

This is just one of dozens of ways to use association. You must understand that when using association that you should always use names of people who are generally liked and respected in the area you're in.

You can also use the name of a fellow co-worker of your potential new customer.

Example: "Janice, you work with Sarah am I right? Well Sarah buys from me all the time."

You can use the company name of your wholesaler if it's well known and gives an impression of quality. How about using the name of someone also in your line of business that people know and respect? You can associate your name with theirs and literally build your own reputation off of their reputation, if they don't mind that is.

Association is extremely powerful. Why do you think big companies spend millions on celebrity and athlete endorsements? These companies want to associate themselves with these big names and build up the image of their product or service.

Since you don't have a huge marketing and advertising budget you can still use the same principle in your business; the same technique on a smaller scale. If you take your time to think about how to use this, its possibilities are almost endless.

It's *OK* to say, "*No!*"

As hard as you try to please your customers and the more breaks you try to give them, sometimes it's just not going to be worth it. Only you know where this limit is and you should be firm with keeping it.

People are just that, people. Most are good and will work with you for a solution to a problem or meet you halfway in a negotiation, but some expect you to give them the World and they won't settle for less.

Just know that it's ok to say no. If your customer or client cannot and will not be satisfied regardless of what you do there is nothing wrong with ending your business with them. Looking at it again from a long-term perspective – if they are this way now, is it worth dealing with this type of person or business a year or two from now?

Again this is a judgment call only you can make, but just know that having limits to what you will and won't do is very necessary. We all hate to turn down business but sometimes it cannot be avoided. If you let them get away with it, then they may bring someone to you who will demand the same thing. All of this can add up to more stress and a bigger headache then its worth.

It's ok to say no. You're in business to make money not to kiss everyone's ass.

Simplifying Networking – The Foundation to Empire Expansion

What is networking exactly? Well I could give you the standard definition, but as you know by now, I'm here to keep things plain and simple, not complex.

"Everything you have to do, everything you want to accomplish involves other people. So get to those people or have them come to you."
- W. James Dennis

Networking is simply helping other people who have the power, resources and ability to help you too. Simple isn't?

In my opinion a golden rule in Networking is this – "Talk means very little, action is king". This goes for both you and them. You both should deliver and respect the Game. A proper business relationship is the coming together of two equal parties.

These people can be fellow Hustlers in your industry or market, owners of other businesses, city or government officials or even your customers who have some pull themselves or know people who do.

Have you ever heard of the theory of, *Six Degrees of Separation*? Well this theory states that you are only six or less people away from meeting anyone you want to meet in the world. Person #1 knows Person #2 who knows Person #3 who knows Person #4 who knows Person #5 who knows the person you want to meet.

Now I can't say I whole-heartedly accept this theory, but the basic principle of it is true. People know other people. And those people know more people. Isn't this how social media sights work online?

Effective Networking is a lot like moving up the Money Chain. Except instead of going after more money, you're going after people who you can help, and who can help you. The more influential the person or people, the higher on the chain you are.

Many of the larger cities have functions and/or meetings that are geared toward nothing but Networking. Fellow business owners all come together to talk and mingle, exchange business cards, etc. They can be fairly difficult to find so you may need to talk to other business owners to see if they go to these functions and would be kind enough to get you an invite. You must understand that these things are almost like a private club, and they don't just let anyone attend; at least in my city.

Networking properly can get you involved in all kind of opportunities. So many I couldn't even list them here. But the bottom line is always two things:

(1) You will be able to make more money because of your new connections.

(2) You may learn ways to save money, because your area of influence will expand. People usually look out for people who look out for them. There are discounts and freebies to be had. Get at them.

Just ponder on the possibilities – you may find new suppliers who will give you a better price. You may run across someone who can get you reasonable deals on advertising. You may meet people who do web design or graphic design. The key here is bartering, not just goods and services either, ideas can also be bartered. You offer something, they offer something. They do a good job and you refer them to people you know. And if they are honest business people, they will do the same for you.

The strategy is similar to the bird dog but instead you will be discounting your products or services for discounted products or services in exchange. Also there is always the potential for more business.

Now this strategy isn't just limited to business owners, it can be done with anyone who has the power, resources and the ability to help you. It could be that geeky kid in high school who will do your web site for free just as long as you tell people about his service.

It can be the young woman who just graduated college with a degree in Business Administration who is looking for work. You may know someone who can help her and in exchange she may do some free business consultation for you and give your business a "tune-up".

It's been said one of the biggest differences between entrepreneurs and employees is that they take risks and they actively seek out and recognize opportunities. Networking is the recognition of the potential that can happen with other people.

Remember the exchange should also be of value and fair. Both parties should feel as though they gained something and came out winners. And if you are a person of your word, your very name itself will begin to gain a reputation. And with that reputation of your name, people will recognize your business. See how that works?

It's 70% about you and 30% about your business when it comes to Networking. People, who are intelligent, will make it a point to surround themselves with similar minded people. So once again, like I've told you from the beginning, sell yourself first and your product and what you do later.

When it comes to Networking always look for any and every opportunity to help others who can help you. That person you help may be able to bring you so much business that you can't keep up, and if nothing else, your name and reputation gets into the social pipeline. People do business with trustworthy and dependable people; if that is your reputation then you will get more business, there's no way you won't. People with solid reputations are fairly rare.

The Up-sell & The Back-End Profit Techniques

Money made from an initial sale (also called point of purchase) is called a front-end sale. Using that sale to sell another product or service leads to what's called the back-end. And it's in the back-end that you can see more profit for the same amount of work.

There is another profitable technique called an up-sell. When you go to a fast food restaurant and order a hamburger the employee behind the counter may ask you, "Would you like fries or a drink with that?" How about when you go to rent a car, don't they always ask you if you would like to add on insurance? Or how about when you go buy a high-end electronic item, such as a television, don't they usually ask you if you want an extended warranty and/or insurance? These are called up-sells.

Up-sell: Turning a single front-end sale into two or more at the point of sale. The up-sell should relate to the initial product or service that is being sold.

Now on to back-ends. Back-ends are usually offered as part of a comprehensive package or as an extension that generates continued revenue. Back-end sales are a form of funneling, keeping the customer is your business loop.

Easy example: You install a pool in your back yard. If the pool company is smart, they not only offer you insurance on the pool pump (up-sell), but they also offer a maintenance service that will come out to check your pool and it's equipment, perhaps even maintain the proper PH balance of the water for you. This service is continual for the life of your pool. You pay for this service either monthly or in some other form of installment plan.

Another easy example: If you were a mobile manicurist you could go to client's homes, do their nails for a front-end fee, and set-up a monthly payment plan where you come and do fill-in work and repair chipped nails at no additional cost. These "maintenance" services are covered in their monthly plan. The client only pays another front-end fee when they want their nails completely re-done with a new design. This concept could work with a mobile pet grooming service as well.

Back-end: A front-end sale that leads to another sale that generates a form of continuous revenue. The continued revenue should relate to the initial product or service being sold (there are some exceptions of course).

In your business, constantly look for ways to offer a little something extra, for a little something more. You already have the customer there; they are already willing to spend money with you so, by just asking, you can increase your profit margin. Like I said simple, isn't it?

Always design your business with either back-end or up-sell products or services in mind. If you can, do both. If you can get up to 10% of the customers to agree, you are more than good. Accomplish this and you are well on your way to making more profit in less time with less work and minimal risk. Isn't that what we all want?

The Worst Enemy of Your Business (Other Than Taxes)
You!

I'm being serious here. Only you can stop yourself. And only you can set yourself up for success or failure. I can write a book filled with a thousand pages and none of it means anything if you don't *use* what's inside.

I considered putting this in the chapter of "Tool#1 – The Mind", but I thought it would be more appropriate here since this is a chapter on strategy.

This is Mental Mathematics, and this is strategy. Remember: Thoughts + Actions = Results

I have given you a lot of basic concept about business that can lead you to your road of success. We have a few more things to discuss in this book, but by reading up to this point you know more about starting and operating a business than 85% of the population. And this is not an exaggeration.

You are your own worst enemy when it comes to business. Yes there are external factors but in the end, how you deal with these will determine the outcome.

Being in business takes a lot of work and the majority of it is mental. Yes you need a lot of steady cash flow, customers, good customer service, good location, good quality product or service, effective marketing and so on and so on. But the very heart of the business, the very soul of it comes from you.

If you're not focused your business will only get so far regardless of how good those other external and material aspects are. You'll make mistakes but don't let that stop you. You'll face what some call competition but you can't let that discourage you. Your business starts and stops with you. Even a bad business partnership can be bounced back from. It was once said that a good person can be completely wiped out financially and come back and make another fortune. Imagine the mental fortitude of an individual like this.

Never focus on your mistakes, learn from them but don't focus on them. Make the necessary adjustment and keep moving. The longer you're in business the easier the basics will become. Once you've mastered the basics, then go on and learn the things that will advance and take you further.

CHAPTER 10
Simplifying Modern Marketing

Marketing is a very intricate subject. So much so that I can't go into great detail in the room we have. I will, like always, give you enough to get you started in the right direction. This is one of the most single important aspects in business. Without effective marketing no one will know about you. And if no one knows about you, you won't make any money. It's like buying the most expensive Mercedes but never driving it because you keep it in the garage, what's the point?

First let us clearly define what marketing is. Many people confuse marketing and advertising. Some people think they are one in the same. They are not.

Advertising is a slice of beef. Marketing is the whole cow. Advertising is the engine and marketing is the whole car. What am I getting at? Advertising is a small portion of marketing. Marketing involves research, testing, and an understanding of people's spending habits, demographics, current trends and how to effectively break your message through to the buying public. After you figure out your message and who it should go to, then advertising delivers that message.

With marketing you identify the target, aim and shoot. You then rely on the force of the advertising shot to "kill" your target.

Not knowing how to properly market your brand (or not doing it at all) will break you. There's no way around it. We've already covered some basic advertising techniques in the last chapter such as what to do with your business cards and/or flyers as well as the bird dog. These are very powerful in themselves, but they are only a part of a much larger strategy.

The best way to understand marketing is to understand what it really is. Marketing involves its own principles which we'll go into here. Again don't be turned off by its simplicity. You're about to learn some powerful marketing information that even people who have degrees in marketing don't know. Marketing as it's taught now is actually an out-dated model. With the speed that life moves now, it's important to go back and understand the buyer's mind in this modern day and time. Things have changed and so must our business strategies.

Marketing is a process, not a one shot deal. It's the building up of your personal image and the image of your business in the minds of the public in general. I say personal image because as a "little guy" or "little gal", you cannot afford to be a cold faceless company.

Now, while you build up this image, you must also direct your marketing to your potential customers, i.e. the people who have a problem you can solve.

The best description of marketing that I have ever come across comes from entrepreneur, *Bruce A. Berman.* If I showed you a regular glass of water and asked you what it was, you would more than likely look at me like an idiot. A glass of water is a glass of water. Now let's pour that glass of water into a nice champagne glass. Next we will add a few drops of red food coloring. We will follow that by putting a slice of orange on the rim and finally we will put in a little paper umbrella. Now what is it? Or rather, what does it *look* like?

If you're honest you would say it looks like a tropical drink. Same water, dressed up to change the **perception** of those who look at it. Think about that, because this is the essence of marketing. The understanding of this principle is what will shape our marketing and advertising efforts.

Second Key; Second Lock

The current school of marketing thought has it wrong. Marketing and advertising is not persuasion. It is conversion. Marketing and advertising is the art of bringing people over to your way of thinking. You want them to see you, your company, the product, service or idea the way *you* want them to see it. You are not trying to convince anyone of anything, you are setting the stage so they can convince themselves.

Now, how is that done? First we must understand a little bit about human psychology.

Let's say I placed you in the Nevada desert, and took away your Identification cards, cell phone, all your jewelry, all your cash, credit cards and debit cards – meaning I left you there with nothing except the clothes on your back and the shoes on your feet. I then told you that you had to make it to New York City and you had three days to do it. How does this scenario make you feel? A little stressed or perhaps gives you a slight sense of hopelessness? How about your thoughts? Where does your mind immediately go?

One of your first thoughts would be on how you could replace what was **lost**. Or in this scenario, what was **taken** from you. A few of your next thoughts would naturally cycle through everything that you **cannot** do because of your lack of resources. Your mind would attempt to find a solution to the problem by first going over what is *not* possible. This is called negation and it is human psychology at its most basic.

But what is the real root problem of this scenario? Lack of money? Lack of time? Lack of food and water? We can find our answer by changing this scenario slightly.

Same as before –You still need to get to New York City, you still have three days to get there and I take away all your possessions. One change this time though, I give you a thousand dollars in cash.

Now how do you feel? Probably not as stressed and hopeless as before, I'm sure. Why? Because you have money in your pocket now and your mind has more to work with in terms of solving the problem. What changed? Both your thoughts and feelings on the situation changed because having cash in your pocket gives you more options. The root of the problem has everything to do with your lack of options. Lacking resources limits your **options**.

The mind is naturally drawn to what pleases it, but you perceive a lack of options because the options you do formulate are unpleasant and therefore quickly discarded.

As technology advances we have a desire to keep up. Most of us do not want to fall behind the curve. Everyone else has a smart phone, we want one too. Everyone else has their own personal stage on social media; we want to have our own stage too. If we don't, we feel as though we're missing out on something. When we are behind, we have limited options.

Hustlers know this basic truth about human nature – Human beings may not try to win, but they don't want to lose.

Winning implies playing harder than everyone else. It's like that co-worker that does just enough to get the job done. He or she isn't trying to win, but they know they have to do just enough to not be fired.

Most people want to take the easiest route; the path involving the least amount of effort. We see this all the time. Every few months there is a new diet pill or supplement. They all promise ridiculous results, for very little effort.

If you think about it you will find hundreds of examples of the, "Little effort for big gains!" marketing ploy.

Now why are human beings like this? Because everything in life **takes** from us. Our jobs take our time, energy and attention. So do our children, our mates, our family and friends. Very few things in our lives actually **give**. So we try to give to ourselves. Convincing someone that a pill will make them lose 15 pounds is not that difficult. They want to believe it. They want to feel something out there can **give** without **taking**. This is why a Hustler must always deliver.

Marketing has changed. People are not paying attention anymore! Did you know that we are inundated with at least five-hundred advertising messages a day? And out of these five-hundred messages we only pay attention to 5%? And out of these 5% we only actually remember five or six advertisements. You don't have to take my word on this; you can verify this by watching yourself throughout the day. How many advertisements do you pay attention to?

All these companies are "yelling" at us, trying to get our attention so they can get their message across. Television, radio, online, on our cell phone apps and games, billboards, signs posted on streetlamps at busy intersections and I could go on and on. The mind filters a lot of this out. We will only pay attention to what is relevant to us.

Being yelled at with advertising does not work anymore. Our attentions are elsewhere. And where is this attention at? On ourselves. We want **options** that require little effort from us. This allows us to comfortably give to ourselves because everything else is taking.

This is why having a personal touch in your business is so important. It levels the playing field with the "Big Boys". There is a face to your company while they are just a name. While they spend millions branding their name, you will spend only thousands, branding yourself. Like I've said before; you first, your business second.

Welcome to the new age of marketing. Jump in, the water is fine.

Now that we have an understanding of an average consumer, let's get into some marketing and advertising basics.

1) The Mind Has It

The mind of the customer is all powerful. It's the customer's mind that makes the decision, and that decision determines where the money goes. Once a customer's mind is made up about something, it's nearly impossible to change.

If you or your business is viewed negatively, then this image will stick. If you give poor customer service and grow a reputation for that, it will stick. Reversing this is very difficult as a small business. The customer's viewpoint on things is not necessarily right or wrong, it just is what it is. So the big thing you need to learn here is:

Once you start out a certain way, you must stay that way. The key word here is consistency! You'll read this a few times throughout this book because I want you to remember it – Never set a pace you can't keep up!

To get a good idea of how this works look at how a tarnished reputation has destroyed the images of many huge companies and the people who have run them. Remember the Enron scandal years ago? Even famous actors and entertainers are not immune. Once they get a bad reputation that usually sticks. People don't look at them in the same light.

The mind of the public is what counts in business. If you can establish yourself in their minds as a professional and expert in your industry you will stay there, unless you do something to change it. Start one way and stay that way.

The buying public's mind is like a file cabinet. It keeps a detailed log of people, businesses and the reputation attached to them. When they hear or see the names, they immediately pull the file and what's in that file is their **perceived** truth.

Marketing is a mental game. Your job is to walk into the customer's mind and make a place there. You can't run in, you have to walk. Running is no longer effective in this new age of marketing. Be clear and concise with your message, but not pushy or over-bearing. You want to appear unique and different. You must separate yourself from everyone else. People won't take the time to wade through details, let your message be short, quick and effective, but also genuine. It can take years to create a positive reputation and only days to destroy it. Keep this in mind as you create your marketing campaigns.

2) Perception – Not Product or Service

What the buying public **perceives** is accepted as the truth, even if it isn't. The best product or service doesn't always win out in the long run. Why is this? Because although it may truly be the best, it's not **perceived** as the best. The Game of business can be cold if you don't understand it.

Marketing is not about selling your product or service (that is advertising). Marketing is about finding a place in the buyer's mind. You do not get there by trying to prove why you're the best. You get there by changing the buyer's perception that you can solve their problem. It just so happens that you have a product or service to do it.

Marketing is a battle of perception first. The actual product and service comes second. Remember our "water into a tropical drink" example from earlier?

Does McDonalds truly have the best tasting fast food? Although this is a subjective question, I would go on to say that most of you would answer no. But the perception of McDonalds is so strong that it really doesn't matter. McDonalds is a fun place; a place to take your children. Sure they have some healthy choices on their menu, but I'm quite sure their basic burgers and fries still sell better than anything else. As long as they never stray too far from their basic menu, this perception will remain. Perception rules the buyer's mind and that mind is the one that makes the decision who gets their money. I just thought that needed to be repeated.

3) Less Is More

As your business grows, it's quite natural to want to add more products or services to what you do. This may be great in the short-term, but in the long-term it can literally cause your business to weaken.

Once again it boils down to perception. The buying public believes you can do one thing well but it's hard for them to believe you can do three, four or five things well. Again, is this right? Maybe it's not, but I'm just here to tell you how it is. This is the reality that every business must face if it is to continue to grow.

Do you remember Xerox computers? Probably not. Xerox is a company known mainly for its copy machines. Why don't you see any Xerox computers today? Because the buying public didn't believe that Xerox could make both copiers and computers well. Their perception had spoken and Xerox computers failed just as fast as it started.

Another example: Remember the "new" coke that came out decades ago? What happened there? You guessed it, they had to bring back the original and rename it Coke Classic. People refused to get used to the taste of something new called Coke. They already loved the original.

How does this apply to you and your business? Simple. The less you do and the better you do it, the easier it is to stay in the forefront of the buyer's mind. I can hear all those so-called experts now. "You need to diversify! The modern market is competitive!" and to be quite honest, there is nothing wrong with diversifying, just don't do completely new things under the same brand. That is what the legal structure of a corporation is for.

Yes, your business needs to grow but don't do it by spreading yourself (and your money) too thin. There is nothing wrong with being known for doing one thing well. If the time ever comes when you want to offer something different, do it under a new name. If you think that sounds crazy then let me ask you a question.

What is the name-brand of Kraft known for? Cheeses. But at the time of this writing, Kraft packages over 50 brands. Over 50! But you don't see Oreo's with the name Kraft sandwich crèmes. You don't see Maxwell House, the coffee, branded as Kraft coffee. Each brand is marketed as a separate entity.

Less is more. Specialization is strong, generalization is weak. Specialization means more money coming from one main source and going back into that source. Generalization means money coming in from multiple sources and going back out to multiple sources. Think of it like an ocean. It's large and slow moving. As the ocean turns into a river it's faster and much more powerful.

Now before we leave this principle let me clarify something. It's ok to diversify a little. It's alright to add services and products that are still within your market or industry. But it must be done correctly. But you'll find, just like these multi-million and billion dollar companies, that what you started out doing will still bring in the majority of your profits 60% - 75% of the time.

4) A Few Words Is All You Need

Businesses come up with fancy slogans and spend thousands on business plans that include fancy mission statements. All of this is great and it does help to focus your business, but the truth is your customer does not care. The only thing that moves them is usually a few words. What are these words? Something that sums up the entire focus of the business. Some quick examples:

What comes to your mind when you think about Volvo? Safety is what comes to mind.

How about Fed-Ex? Overnight usually comes to mind.

How about Microsoft? Software applications usually come to mind (Windows in particular); or PC (personal computer).

We talked earlier about walking into the minds of the customer. And the easiest way to do this is by attaching a word to your business and making that stick. Now, be careful here, again perception rules the day. You can't completely own another word that is already taken. People just won't accept it. You can use it, but you cannot truly own it.

You must take the time to break down what it is you do in business and sum it up into a few words. This isn't easy but it's very necessary for effective marketing. Most of these magic "key-words" are usually a benefit. Something that says ease and effective results works best. Take for example Wal-Mart. Their key-words are Low Prices and Rollback. They are attached to a huge benefit, and that benefit is saving people money as well as convenience.

When you come up with that catchy slogan of yours, be sure that your key-words are in there somewhere. Or you can do like Microsoft and put it in your company name (Microsoft = Micro Computer and Software).

To make these words stick, you must deliver what it is you say you can deliver. And over time your company will be attached to those words. If you can successfully combine your company with a benefit, you have just gone from having a company to creating a brand. And this is the foundation towards bigger business.

A brand is simply a label for your business. It's what your business and its products are attached to. Many brand names become a trademark, which means that no other company can use it. Coca-Cola for example is a company and a brand. The way the name is displayed is its trademark.

You need to keep these things in mind before you start your business or at the very least, before you start making your way up the Money Chain. Tie your company to a few words. Tie those words to a brand. And tie your brand to a trademark (or make your brand your trademark). It works like this – When people see your trademark, they should immediately think about your brand and your company.

Uncommon Marketing Wisdom – The Lion and the Monkey

The lion is fierce, territorial and the king of all he surveys. There are few that can challenge him. The monkey is nimble and fast yet possesses no real strength. The monkey is sly and quick; a survivalist. The Lion rules, the monkey mimics. In other words, the lion is the creator and the monkey is a follower. Which are you in your market?

As you study marketing materials and business books in general you will usually hear a lot of the same tired advice.

- "Don't reinvent the wheel!" - "Stick with the winners. Do what they do." - "If you know the recipe and repeat it, you will get similar results."

Any of these sound familiar? And is this good advice? Well, that would depend on you. Are you a lion in business, or a monkey? Sounds silly doesn't it? Well let me explain myself.

As a lion, you are a creator. You may not be creating anything particularly new that has never been seen or heard of before, but you are willing to take risks and try to blaze new trails. As a monkey you are a copy-cat so to speak, you mimic the actions of those stronger than yourself and only go places you feel are safe and familiar.

A copy of something is never as good as the original. What this means in marketing is that if you are copying a leader (lion), you will almost never remove him from his position (territory). A copier will always be number two or higher. Why? Because in the customer's mind, the lion (number one) is the original and viewed as the authority.

Do you remember the winner of the bronze medal in an Olympic event? Very rarely. But you do remember the gold medal winner.

Let's see this in the real world. Let's take McDonalds and Burger King. Both are fast food restaurants and both sell hamburgers, fries, sodas and shakes among other similar things. Now, in overall sales, who's number one? Easy right? McDonalds wins hands down. But did you know there was a time when Burger King was closing the gap between themselves and McDonalds? The monkey was putting pressure on the lion. How did they do that?

Everything has an opposite aspect. Loud and quiet, hot and cold, sharp and dull, etc. In marketing this is true as well. You will have a hard time forcing the lion out of his territory, but you can get your own territory and become the lion there.

What Burger King did was take the *opposite* position in the fast food burger world. What was McDonalds main marketing strategy geared towards? The answer was the children (at the time it was at least). Burger King took the marketing position of pointing that out. McDonalds was "kiddy land" so they made themselves the place for grown-ups. See how that works?

Burger King stopped copying McDonalds and developed a territory of their own. And it worked pretty well too. Now why they stopped doing that, I have no idea, but their current market share reflects them going back to playing the monkey.

Everyone wants you to follow the leader, but when the leader started, who did they have to copy? That's right, **nobody**!

I shared all this with you to get you to think. You don't always have to follow the leader. You will not always be able to pinpoint your demographics and the market you're trying to sell to. You may not get it right the first time, and that is fine. As a small business you have the advantage of quickly changing your tactics. You may not get it right the first time, but the Big Boys don't either.

Final word: It's fine to be the monkey and copy the leader if you want to. You will make money and may find your success. Just don't expect to outperform the lion in his own territory. Doing, "Monkey see, Monkey do" will never yield you the "Lion's Share" of the wealth. Do you catch my drift? The customer's perception will almost never let that happen when it comes to a small business.

Now let us move on to where a small business can grow a huge advantage over older established companies. Where current perceptions are easily identified and where you can set the stage the way you want. This new stage is called social media.

CHAPTER 11
The Circle of Social Media

Social Media is currently the number one reason the marketing and advertising landscape has changed so much over the last decade. And thanks to it, almost any small business can jump into the market. This is both good and bad. Now that the barrier for entry is so low, many more people are in the pool. This means that you have to be just that much more unique just to be noticed. The good side of this is now we can market and advertise for little to nothing. We can compete on a level playing field with the Big Boys. Mainly because they haven't quite figured it out yet.

The principles and techniques we will explore in the Social Media arena are similar to the ones we've previously discussed. The principles and concepts in this book are universal. They work regardless of platform. Social Media (noted as SM from this point forward) is a great stage, where you are the star and it just so happens this stage reaches across the world. This is a great time for small business; now let's get into some business Game.

SM, used correctly, fulfills a few basic things for your business. It gives and improves brand awareness, increases visibility, gives you and/or your company a "face" (presence), and it allows you to connect directly to your customers. In fact, you can get feedback on how well you are doing, or not doing, fairly rapidly. This is great because as a small business you can adjust and make changes in very little time.

Why do we enter the SM stage? To create fans. And these fans will spread our brand. SM is the ultimate form of word of mouth advertising! And this advertising reaches across the world. Do you know how much of a budget you would have needed twenty years ago for your brand to reach across the world? Think about it.

I get a lot of question about how to maximize the effect of Social Media and I always say start at square one. What is the number one factor people have as an obstacle to buy from you? Sometimes money is a factor, but there is a larger factor. And that larger factor is trust.

Remember, word of mouth advertising is so effective because people are hearing information and praises from people they already trust. When you say it, it means very little, but when someone they trust says it, it means a lot. This is trust through the principle of association (refer to Chapter Nine).

Your goal on SM is **not** to advertise. It is to build trust. Stop "yelling" out your message, start learning to communicate and listen. We have already established that people are not paying attention to advertising, they have other agendas. So why waste the time? There is a more effective way.

What do you do on SM now? You read the posts by people on your friends list. You post pictures; you share things that you think are funny, clever or newsworthy. You comment, you like and you share. Well guess what? When you're in business you are going to be doing the same exact things, just from the **perspective** of yourself as a business owner. Yes, it is that simple.

Our Hustler, Michael, finds an interesting article about a gentleman in Africa who does some unique never before seen designs on shirts. Michael likes this, comments on it and shares it.

Michael spent twelve hours at his business today, very unusual and he's tired but feeling good. He posts that making sure to mention his company name (and only his company name).

Michael takes a picture of a few shirt designs he is thinking of offering to his customers, he asks his follower's opinions. He honestly begins listening and responding to their comments, establishing an open dialogue.

Michael found a new music band that he likes; he posts a link to their website, makes a comment and shares one of their videos.

Michael's mother comes in town. He hasn't seen her in almost two years. He posts a single picture of them together looking happy during this joyous reunion. He writes about this in his blog and posts a link to that on SM. It just so happens Michael's blog is directly on his website; very convenient.

Michael posts as a real person who just happens to have a business. Not as **just** a business. Yes he includes relevant thoughts, ideas, news and articles that reflect the clothing business (particularly T-shirts and sports caps), but he is a person *first*. This gives a face to your company. It is something the Big Boys cannot do. Unless you are a huge fan or an investor, do you really care what the CEO of a major corporation is doing right now? And would you take your time to listen to him or her without wondering if there was a sales pitch coming?

The formula is easy. 75% of all your posts, regardless of your social platform of choice (Facebook, Twitter, YouTube, Instagram, Tumblr, etc.) should be casual conversation. We want to post and share things that bring us into dialogue with our followers. 20% can be mentions of your business's products or service and announcements. I said mentions and announcements, not advertising! Announcing new products is fine as well, just skip the sales pitch. The remaining 5% is actual advertising.

Out of one-hundred posts on a single SM platform, only five (up to 10) should be actual advertising.

I remember a time when I went to a very well known jewelry store to purchase an item. As standard procedure now-a-days at check out, they asked for my email address and I gave it to them. They emailed me every day with a sales pitch. I am not exaggerating; sometimes it was two or three times a day. Do you know how annoying that was? My cell phone alert is alerting and I go look and it's another jewelry store email telling me about 25% off savings and special deals. You have special deals every day? Good for you, fantastic! I unsubscribed. I don't want to see this in my inbox two to three times a day.

And that was just email, can you imagine if this was a twitter feed or a Facebook news feed? I have to look at your advertisements all day, every day? The chewing gum sort of loses flavor after awhile, am I right? How about something with more substance, like how a jewelry design goes from sketch to finished product? Wouldn't that be more interesting? Especially in video format. Anyway, moving on.

Let's look at the Hustler's way. If Michael were to stock a new shirt design, he would post a picture with a line something like, "New Hotness!" with a link to his website. The photo itself would also have his website address on it so if this picture is shared, he gets free advertising. That is all. Let the website sell it, not the SM platform. And he wouldn't repost this two to three times a day! Twice a week is perfectly acceptable. He also responds to all comments whether they are praises or criticisms. Always in a professional manner and always in a way that keeps the dialogue open-ended. More comments mean more attention, always keep that in mind.

Over time, what does this do? It establishes Michael as an expert or authority in this field. He posts about it often, he shares relevant information about it and he has a website surrounding it. He must know what he's talking about, right? That's trust, and this is what we want, isn't it?

Think of yourself like a mayor on the campaign trail. You're interacting with the public, sharing your ideas and visions and also listening and engaging with your followers. Shake hands and kiss babies – you get the idea. Sincere interaction should be your priority and establishing a clear "brand voice" should be your ultimate goal.

SM also allows us to follow trends, to see where our market is headed. The "Feedback Loop", people commenting on our posts or on posts from other people in our industry, allow us to discover weaknesses in our business model and even check out the competition. All for a little more than a time investment – SM is that powerful.

Engaging and starting conversation is the key to SM. We want to engage with our customers and fans; we want to exchange ideas with them. Isn't that the point of SM anyway? Who tries to make all of this so complicated?

We want to create a community around our brand. Just because it is your stage doesn't mean you hog the spotlight. Just like a face to face sales situation, you want to write 30% - 40% of the time when commenting and let the community do the rest.

If someone in your community offers some stellar feedback, grab it! Repost it, retweet it, create an entire blog post about it. Allow the community to develop its own personality. This is very important. Just like you are trying to establish your own brand voice, the community around your brand will establish its own voice as well. Never discourage that.

Keep all your SM efforts up to date and relevant. This is especially important on Facebook. If you choose to have a Business Page or Fan Page rather than a Personal Page, search engines can actually rank you if you maintain relevant information. This takes work, but it is part of the Grind and therefore necessary in the Game.

Do not be sneaky. Don't try to Tag a headline about something that is trending, but the core of your message is about you. You will kill your credibility quickly. This is a violation of the Game. Keep your integrity. Be the star of your stage, you don't need to use someone else's stage to draw attention to your own.

How much time do you want to dedicate to this? I would recommend being on at least two platforms and having a blog. Always keep your SM posts short and concise and your blog posts between 500 to 750 words or less.

Make sure you take advantage of Cross-Platform-Promotion (CPP). This means simply tying all your SM platforms together. Your blog links to your Twitter, your Twitter links to your Facebook and all of these link to your website and your website links back to all of them. That is the Circle of Social Media. Remember all of this is marketing; it is just not traditional marketing. And like any type of marketing, it is necessary.

Again, this is enough information to get you started in the right direction. Combine these techniques with the other techniques and strategies along with what you just learned on marketing to create a truly powerful brand voice.

At the time of this writing, SM as a marketing platform has still not been figured-out, even the Big Boys will admit to that. I will not claim to have all the answers either, but what I do know from my business experience is that having a company with a "face", and customer interaction contributed tremendously to my success. Nothing replaces social interaction; it is one of our most basic desires (refer to Chapter Nine - Know Your Customers and Know Your Product, Service or Idea).

Have you ever called a customer service number to go through five minutes of menu options only to be placed on hold for fifteen minutes? We just want to talk to someone about our concerns! Why is that so difficult?

People want to be heard. Let them be heard. Create your stage so that everyone wins.

The Social Media Cityscape – From Block to Block

Now that we've had a detailed overview, let's dig a little deeper into what I call the major five. These may not be the best SM platforms for *your* particular business, but to ignore them completely would be reckless. The Big Boys are desperately trying to find a way to conquer the enigma of SM but to me I look at SM like a large city. Each street and block has its own flavor and unique appeal. When you're on an SM site you are literally hanging out on that particular street or block "kickin' it". You're talking to passersby, discovering new and interesting places and getting familiar with the regulars who frequent there.

I want you to imagine the whole of SM as a large city. You have Downtown, Uptown, the wealthy areas and the poor areas. You also have the suburbs. Each SM platform is its own part of the city and each has its own style and expectations.

There are three main ways to communicate on SM – Through visuals, auditory or through writing. Some platforms function well with all three, others are best with one or two. While you make your way around the various parts of "town", you must fit in with the style and culture of the area you're in. If you don't belong there, people will recognize it immediately. Let's examine the SM cityscape.

Facebook – Uptown Slick

The undisputed leader. At the time of this writing Facebook is the social medium of choice for the slightly more mature audience. If your market is the younger crowd (15-21), you are better off on twitter. Teenagers are gradually moving away from Facebook because their parents and grandparents are there. What teenager do you know wants their close family all in their personal business? Facebook's appeal is also its weakness.

Facebook is primarily for writing – Stories work well, sharing experiences and interesting thoughts. Facebook works well visually as well. Meme's (those cute photos featuring scenes from television shows or movies with text captions), links to videos and personal photos. You can be fairly personal on Facebook which really helps with personal branding. Don't be afraid to start conversations and discussions. Hitting on controversial topics works well here as well.

Twitter – Downtown Commotion

Twitter caters to a slightly younger crowd but like Facebook it reaches a good amount of age ranges. Twitter is fast and furious. It's noisy and requires a very interesting approach to be heard. Twitter is primarily a writer's medium and works best to air your feelings and thoughts. Everything else you post should link and point to somewhere else, preferably your website, your Facebook or YouTube channel.

Twitter does not function well in the area of conversation but it is a powerhouse in getting immediate feedback from your brand loyalists (as well as your brand detractors). View it like this: Use insightful comments and observations, share feelings and thoughts, and speak your truth of moment. Twitter is not the place to start conversations or discussions. Meet, greet and keep it moving just like being in the hustle and bustle of a major downtown metropolis.

YouTube – The "Hood"

YouTube is expansive, there is a little of everything to be found here. From how-to videos, to music videos, to tips and tricks on home improvement, if you can't find it here, I would honestly be shocked. It takes a lot to stand out here because there is just so much content for people to sift through. Depending on your business, YouTube is best used as a supplement to Facebook and/or Twitter. The disadvantage of YouTube is it works against the speed of other SM platforms. This has its advantages if used properly. On YouTube you can go into major detail.

YouTube is visual and auditory; this alone makes it a prime choice to give your brand an extremely personal touch. You have to be cautious here though. YouTube is the "hood", and the feedback and comments about your efforts can sometime be pretty harsh. Make sure you have some thick skin because people expect a certain amount of production quality and value.

Another advantage YouTube has that other SM sites do not, is that you can actually partner with Google and receive a kick-back on advertising that you allow on your channel. This can be a nice little income stream if you can maintain a high amount of viewers through consistent content.

Pinterest – Suburban Classy

Pinterest is fantasy land. The fences are white and the grass is always green. Pinterest is largely a visual medium and the audience here is majority women.

When people pin items, they are largely pinning things they want and desire in the future; fashion, jewelry, cars, house wares, etc. They also pin inspirational quotes, recipes and beautiful photos. When you step foot into this part of "town" your voice must be strong, but never overbearing. Always use your manners and make sure what you do is of value. Classy, elegant and beautiful should be your style here.

Instagram – Midtown Swag

Instagram is primarily a visual medium although at the time of this writing you can also post 15 second videos. This is can be very powerful because of its ease and speed. Unlike YouTube people are not expecting a certain level of production value.

Intstagram is a cross between Facebook and Twitter. Fast but not noisy; you can be personal but not have to begin discussions and create conversation. You can communicate through simple visual representations. Swag (unique style) is very powerful here. Similar to Twitter, all your mentioned links should go to your website or Facebook at the very least.

These are my main five but you must find what works best for you.

When you enter the circle of Social Media make sure you step in correctly and always keep in mind why you are there. Be ever so cautious not to blemish your brand through petty online arguments and feeding negativity. This is a violation of the Game.

People want to be heard, let them speak their mind. If you ever find yourself in a situation where you must defend your position (or a decision), do it with grace and with respect to the other person or people who have an issue. If you can gracefully explain your position, most people will understand and respect the fact that you were listening to them. You may not win them over, but you won't damage your reputation either. Either way, you win.

Now let's move on to buyer's psychology – what makes people spend money.

CHAPTER 12
A Big Piece of the Puzzle

Third Key; Third Lock

We have come a long way. By now your mind should be buzzing with ideas and hopefully you should be already formulating plans to either start or expand your business. But before you take those final steps I need to share something with you that you may never hear or read in any other business book. The reason is because people are afraid to talk about it, although it's right in front of their face.

Before I give this information to you let me quickly set you up for it. You really must understand and apply this to yourself *first*, so you can see the truth in what I have to say. We've talked about the power of perception and how that influences people's buying decisions. But these perceptions are just one part of the formula.

We've discussed, in part, that the core of business involves solving problems. But do you know where the money is really at in business? It's in solving people's **emotional** problems. I'm not saying go be a psychologist, I'm saying when people buy, they buy emotionally. They buy what they **feel** they want, not necessarily what they need. Even if what they want is not good for them. If they **perceive** and **feel** it's going to get them the results they want, they will spend money on it.

I'm about to hit you with a lot of business Game so please pay attention.

Perception is King and emotion is Queen. Take that perception and mix it with emotion and what you get is a third quality or attribute. And this attribute is called, "Dependency".

Some may view what I am about to reveal as dark. But I assure you it is necessary. Think of it like taking the red pill in the movie, The Matrix. It will change your paradigm and shatter your current perception of reality.

Entire businesses are built around fulfilling the dependencies of wants, desires and emotions that people have. This understanding and being in a position to satisfy dependency is a key component to business success.

Just what is dependency? Dependency is a need or want so strong, that a person will sacrifice other things in order to obtain it. Dependency can also be a need or want that was once satisfied then **lost** and a person is desperate to get it back.

Don't view dependency as something negative. We depend on the sun to shine every day. We depend on our jobs to allow us to take care of our needs. We depend on the government to remain stable so we can focus on living our lives. We depend on others to be there when we need them the most. If all the cell phone carriers shut down, the world would go into a state of temporary chaos. How about that leaking pipe behind the wall that runs the risk of creating harmful mold? Unless you have the skill, you must depend on someone else to come fix the problem.

The key is dependency, but why? Because people desire a fantasy world; a world where they expect to receive something, a feeling, a satisfaction, a release from pain or worry, etc. without giving a lot of themselves to get it. We talked about this in the marketing chapter. People want the easy and quick way to obtain whatever it is they desire, or the easy and quick way to get away from what they fear. Think about that for a moment.

Understand Game. If you can stage something the correct way so that your customer perceives it the right way, your marketing and advertising will be effective. And this translates into a profitable business. You do not have to resort to any trickery or manipulation to have an effective marketing campaign when you understand dependency.

The following list is not made to offend anyone, but these can be (and are) real dependencies that some people may not even realize they have.

Sexual fulfillment and gratification
Gambling
The desire for easy (and quick) solutions
The desire to look better or younger
The desire for security and/or safety
Wanting to make more money and/or save it
Narcotics, alcohol and/or cigarettes, etc.
Spirituality
The desire to be loved or find love (romance)
The desire to be respected
Food
Clothes and/or shoes

Entertainment (music, movies and novels)
The idea of being someone famous
The idea of being someone important
Learning new things
Television
The internet
Video games

And I could go on but I hope you see my point. Whatever you spend your time doing the most, you're dependent on. Whatever you spend your time thinking about the most, you're dependent on. Whatever you spend your money on the most, you're dependent on.

FACT: People give their time, energy and money to things that are important to them. If you can identify where a person's time, energy and money go, you can pinpoint their dependency. Before you begin to think about how this applies to someone else, apply this to yourself *first* so you can truly understand the power of what you're reading.

If someone has a strong enough dependency (a want they will sacrifice other things for), then they can be sold and funneled. By funneling I mean, they stay in your business loop and continue to spend money with you.

A person can even be addicted to working (a workaholic) or decorating their home. Do you go out of your way in the morning to get that "special" brand of coffee? These are the forms of the dependency I'm speaking of.

Again, none of this has to do with an actual product or service, only in the way it makes you feel when you get it and/or use it. Let's look at it again.

You pay money to get problems solved. Can we agree on that? Now, when these problems are solved, you have received a fulfillment of a desire. Can we agree on that? In return for this fulfilled desire, you get a certain feeling inside. And it's these desires that lead to the feeling of want that can possibly become a dependency. Not the actually fulfillment itself!

Why do I say this? Simple. The fulfillment of a desire would be just that, **fulfillment**. It would end and stop there. But if you continually have the desire and that feeling of want, then that is dependency. You will go back again and again to fulfill that same desire. I hope I'm not losing you here.

Your next question should be, "Where do these dependencies come from?"

The answer is that they come from the things people see every day. The things they covet. Again, they do not like to feel like they are losing, or left out. People are never satisfied, they will always want something. They will often place these wants ahead of their needs. The truth is, wants are never satisfied, one leads to another and then another. It's like being online. You start out looking up one topic and two hours later you find yourself looking at something that has nothing to do with the originally topic you went online for.

Big business knows this but will never admit it. It's the foundation of any successful business. This principle is barely represented or non-existent in businesses that fail. Big business spends billions of dollars a year trying to play into our emotions and desires because if they can get you "hooked", they may just have a lifetime customer.

You know this is true of yourself because you have favorite things. You have a group of favorite restaurants, you have a dream car in mind, you have a circle of favorite television shows, favorite singers or bands and you have a favorite genre of movie. And all these things have nothing to do with the actual product or service itself, it all has to do with you and how these things will make you feel when you have them! Try to get that sports fanatic to go an entire year with no cable or satellite sports coverage and see what happens!

All these things bring you a certain feeling and it's that feeling that keeps you going back again and again. It's so much a part of you that it requires little thought anymore. About 50% to 75% of the things you buy, you are addicted to in some form or fashion. The rest of the things you buy are almost purely out of habit. Let's pause here a moment. I want you to think a minute and let all this sink in.

The businesses that do the best are the ones that answer the call of dependency and do it well. Dependency is like a blank music CD. It can be "burned" with these feelings and desires of want and then played in your mind. Sometimes it goes on repeat and it plays over and over again. Eventually you will get tired of hearing it and go get that feeling (desire) fulfilled.

Desire (the emotion/feeling of want) **+ Perception** (who or what will best fulfill that desire) **+ A business** (the ability to fulfill the desire) **= Money**

Without any fluff from me all I can tell you is that dependency equals money. There's no way else to say it. Even trying to avoid dependency *is* a dependency because it is a strong desire.

There are a lot of various types of businesses out there and each one caters to specific needs and wants. But let's go away from individual businesses for a moment and look at actual industries. These are some of the biggest industries in the world right now, in no particular order. There are more of course, but these are among the top 25.

Food
Housing
Clothing
Transportation (including vehicles, petroleum, etc.)
Technology (including computers, software, cell phones, etc.)
Alcohol
Tobacco
Adult oriented entertainment (including pornography, classes, magazines, etc.)
General entertainment (including music, movies, stage plays, etc.)
Funeral services

Each and every one of these industries serves an emotional desire. Even if the desire itself is to avoid pain or loss. Not having a vehicle for instance can cause great pain if you live in an area where public transportation doesn't exist.

As a small business owner you are in no position to control an entire industry so you must make due with a small share of it. But even just half of one percent (0.50) of a multi-billion dollar industry is an excellent place to start.

When you look at your business you can't just see **only** your business. You must look at the industry as a whole. Since you are now (or will soon be) placing yourself inside an industry you need to have an understanding of how it works, what your industry is about and equally important, where the money is going. Again, if you can follow the money you can find the major dependency point.

Once you find the dependency point, either copy it and improve upon it, or niche it to a new market within the industry by changing up a few things. This is where many business owners make their mistake. They niche their product or service, but they usually niche the wrong thing to the wrong market. They didn't find the point of dependency first!

Let's look at a real world example. Apple computers were one of the first companies to niche the computer for home use. They weren't the first, but they were successful in becoming known as *the* home computer to have.

Did they invent the computer? No. Did they invent the concept of computers and what they could do? No. But what they did was saw a future need. A need for people at home to have the power of using a computer. It was a niche then, now we can't imagine life without a computing device in one form or another.

How about that ever so popular book series known as, <u>Chicken Soup for the Soul</u>? This book series was expanded to include separate books for teenagers, business owners, etc. One industry, the book industry. A main product properly marketed to build perception and value. Then by using the name alone, it was niche to specific groups (demographics) of people. Brilliant! What's the dependency point here? These books are a collection of inspirational stories. People who are dependent on inspiration, wisdom, self-growth and awareness eat this type of material up.

You however don't necessarily need to begin this way. You can go straight for the niche. Just remember, work your niche off of your industries main dependency point. This takes some time and research but by doing this you greatly increase your chances of success right out the gate. Just follow the money.

A quick word here. There is, was and will always be fads. Things that are popular for a year or two and then fade away into history. Do not base your business on a fad or what's cool. Plant the seeds of your business in the ground of the overall established industry. When you have the money to jump in and invest in a fad idea, then do so. Just realize that you cannot build a long-term business on a fad. Get on the fad horse and ride it until you can't anymore.

I was once asked how to apply the idea of dependency to a Cleaning Service business. The woman I was speaking with very much understood what I was saying about points of dependency but couldn't quite see how it applied to a Cleaning Service.

She went on to tell me that possibly she chose the wrong business to begin her entrepreneurial career and looked slightly discouraged. I assured her that everything was just fine. The cleaning service industry is a multi-hundred million dollar a year industry, how is that a wrong decision? She went on to say that she just didn't understand what would move people to come and do business with her over a bigger more established company. She also didn't understand how she should market a dependency in a service that didn't seem to have one.

I listened patiently and smiled. She understood the idea, but she didn't know how to translate it to her business. I asked her a couple of questions.

"Why do you think people pay to have their businesses and homes cleaned?"

She answered, "Well, I guess they don't have the time or are too lazy to do it for themselves," I nodded and then went on to my next question, "So if people are willing to pay for the privilege, don't you think having a spotless home or business is important to them?"

"Yes, I mean if they're paying it must be important. But I still don't see a point of dependency there," she said.

I smiled and shook my head. I went on to explain to her that the point of dependency had very little to do with the service itself. People want to save time and impress people. Having a clean home and business is very impressive to guests and clients. It shows caring and attention to detail, it also shows that the person or business is on top of their Game. Not only that, it is a huge time saver.

The dependency points in a Cleaning Service are about gaining time, avoiding the discomfort of doing it themselves and being presentable while avoiding embarrassment. These desires are so strong, that they are willing to pay for it. She was literally saving people *from* themselves. Without her, they would gain little in the way of time, appearance and possibly set themselves up for humiliation.

Needless to say she lit up like a light bulb. Once she grasped what I told her she then immediately knew how to market her service in such a way that it would reach people on the emotional level. Giving them what they really wanted from her service, the simple desire to save themselves a headache.

So now take the time to think about how to use this information to start or improve your current business. Look beneath the actual products, services or ideas. Properly used, this is the key to bigger profits. Dependency comes in all shapes, sizes and forms and are what your marketing efforts should be based around. Subtly let people know that you can give them those feelings that they long for and you can do it better (and maybe cheaper) then the next person. Use this and you will be astounded by the returns you get from it.

"You don't have to chase the fox. Put all your chickens in one bunch and the fox will come to you."
– Old Hustler saying

To help you on your way I have yet another list for you. This one outlines the 12 most basic dependency points. There are more, but as always, these are enough to get you started. Each one can be viewed two different ways. People will either want them, or people are trying to avoid them; or more specifically, the negative aspects of them. People want something (gain) and people are afraid of something (avoidance).

Food, for example, is a need. Great tasting food is a want, yet there are people who only want the healthiest of food so they avoid certain types of food altogether, regardless of how good it may taste.

The powers of this list are in the combinations. Like the healthy eater in our example above is in two categories, Food (1) and Living Better (10). A person may use a Social Media platform to communicate and maintain relationships (5), entertain themselves (7) but also to receive just a little admiration for their wit and great sense of humor (11). After all, we all want to be heard.

Gain and avoidance work with the combinations as well. A person can avoid sex (6) because they feel it will help them gain a sense of mental and emotional well-being (8). If you seriously take your time and go through the list, you will be amazed at what you will see.

(1) Food
(2) Clothing
(3) Shelter
(4) Security/Safety
(5) Communication/Relationships
(6) Sex
(7) Entertainment
(8) Mental and Emotional Well-Being/Spirituality
(9) Wealth/Saving Money
(10) Living Better (health/medicine)
(11) Admiration/Power /Prestige
(12) Convenience

CHAPTER 13
Final Words and Thoughts

Thank you for taking your time to read this material. This work is a combination of many years of mentorship, study, trial and error. I realize that a lot of this material may be completely new to you and you probably want a place to start. Be patient with me a little longer we'll go over that in our last chapter.

We've covered a lot of information in a very short time. And just to think, this only scratches the surface of the many techniques and business principles I've learned. I am often asked is there just one secret to business success and I have to reply, "No, there isn't."

Everything we covered is important as a whole. You may not need to personally use all the information, but it's all part of a way of thinking. The Hustler's way of thinking.

Along with the information presented here you will also need to understand asset protection, basic business law (so you don't get screwed or screw yourself), a basic understanding of banks and financing, proper business structure and organization, contractual agreements, the difference between assets and liabilities as well as the difference between having money and having a net worth.

The important thing to remember with all of this is to keep things as simple as possible. Any person, book, class or seminar that won't do that is wasting your time. Not only do you have to study it, but you then have to go back and understand it. Shouldn't it be simple enough to at least make sense the first time around?

Sure, you're going to be learning new concepts and terminologies but in the end it shouldn't give you a headache. In everything I do, I make it a point to simplify and streamline it. In other words, I try to get to the source or root of the information as quickly as possible.

Another point to keep in mind as you begin doing business is that in order to make more money, you will have to help more people.

Your income will at some point "even out" so to speak. As much as you work, when that time comes and you look at your profits, you will see that you are bringing in about the same amount of money. This means it's time to turn up the volume! Get back into your marketing efforts, run those bird dog programs. Have you been using cards and flyers? Well now it may be time for print ads in the local paper or industry magazines (depending on your business), even a radio spot. In essence, put back the same energy into your business that you did when you started.

The more people you reach, the more you can help and the more profit there is to be had. In business, never get too comfortable where you're at. Keep pushing. Keep moving. Don't let your business momentum die out or slow down. I've made this mistake before; please don't make it one of your own.

Once your business is successful enough to provide a comfortable lifestyle then it's time to learn about investing and building residual (passive) income. If you don't do this, then you will always be just a business owner. And a business owner does nothing but own a "job". Do your best not to get trapped here if at all possible. Owning a business is rewarding, but it's one of many steps to being truly financially free.

Also I need to mention here that persistence is very much needed through all of this. You must stay focused and be persistent. There may be times when your profits for a month or two look terrible. Don't give up just yet. Just examine what you're doing and see if there is something you can improve on.

Maybe you're marketing is all wrong. Maybe your price points are off. The best way to judge what to improve is to simply ask for feedback from your customers. Never give up on an idea until you have exhausted every possible angle and made improvements.

Of course, having a nice sized business budget helps in this area too. But if you don't have that, then you may need to throw in the towel early. Don't lose what you already have (home, vehicle, etc.) and take money from it to fuel your business. There are of course exceptions to this rule, business is risk after all. In fact I've broken this rule a few times. But if you can't manage it then there is no shame in holding off for a while or even starting over; although this can be painful.

Also get a website up if possible. People are under the **perception** (there's that word again) that websites can be very expensive to set up. And if you're not thinking with a Hustler's mind by now, that would be true.

Can you accept the fact that there are middle school and high school kids out there that know almost as much about computers, programming and design as professionals with degrees? And don't you think it's possible to track these people down and ask them for their help? Perhaps you can do something for them in return. A small payment, maybe just help them get their name out as web-site designer. If you can work it right, you may be able to get it done for free. All of this is Networking.

Websites for a business used to be a luxury, now it's a necessity. Since the perception of web sites is that they are expensive, if you have one, you only look more legitimate and professional.

It doesn't need to look pretty; it doesn't need to have a whole bunch of bells, buttons and whistles (unless of course you run a design type business) all it needs to do is contain information about you and your company. Add a couple of pictures and you're in there.

Another thing that you may want to consider is getting a hold of a mentor. Preferably someone in your industry that can help keep you inspired and can pass on their knowledge and experience to you. This isn't always possible, but if you can find one they can save you time, money and frustration.

Finally, move fast, but don't rush. Make sure you do diligent research and make it a point to understand things thoroughly, to best of your ability, before committing to them.

Would you marry someone who you just met a day ago? I hope you said no. You would of course want to take the time to get to know this person. You would want to know what they stand for, and who they are. You would want to see if they were compatible with you and your goals. It's the same thing in business.

Sure we make bad judgment calls in our love relationships and it's just as easy to do in business. But it's better to gather the facts and then commit to a decision, then not to do anything at all. If it doesn't work out, it just doesn't work out. That's life in general. When it comes to the legal aspects of business, I would advise to be even more cautious. You can screw your finances up pretty bad if you don't know what you're doing.

I said that not to scare you, but to get you to slow down just a bit and try not to overlook too much. Again, don't take a year in research mode, but make sure you do an adequate job. Then when you think it makes sense, commit, decide and go for it!

Are you still there? Good! We're almost done.

CHAPTER 14
Stepping Out – Starting Your Business Step-By-Step

Opening the First Door

So here we are, at the end of our journey. For those of you who have yet to start your enterprise, here is a step-by-step roadmap to implement a lot of what we've covered. Please make note that this may need to be altered and changed to fit your particular business so I'll keep it very general. Take what you need and develop from there.

When I started my first couple of businesses I had no knowledge, no mentor and no clue as to what I was doing. Fortunately I ran across people who were willing to educate me and point me in the right direction. I still made my share of mistakes, I have my bumps and bruises, but my passion and desire kept me going. Let that be the same with you.

Business, just like life, isn't easy – but it doesn't need to be complicated. Whenever I start a new enterprise, these are the steps I follow.

"Keep it moving and keep it simple in the process."
- W. James Dennis

1) Begin Hustler's Math

Start doing everything in your power to save that 10% to 20%. This is the money you are going to use to begin your enterprise. Remember, don't touch it! If necessary put it in a separate bank account. If you are already knowledgeable in investments and you can do them with little risk then by all means flip that money to speed up the process.

2) The Idea

To enjoy what you do is very important. It's really amazing that almost anything now-a-days can be turned into a business. Analyze your talents and skills. Make a list of things you know how to do. And I do mean everything! Can you believe walking, marketed as low-impact exercise, is a multi-million dollar a year industry?

3) On To the Research

Narrow your talents and or knowledge down to five or ten things. Then either go to the library, bookstore or Google away online and look for information, websites, magazines, books, etc that you can find on your talents. You are looking for the point of dependency. Remember, follow the money. Look at the corporations and business owners doing it big in the field. Look at how they market and if possible get some of their products. Study them and determine whether you can do this yourself in your own way.

4) Determine Your Strategy

So what is it going to be? Lion or monkey? Are you going to follow the leader or niche your product to the area the Big-Guys missed? Decide on an area and commit to it.

This could be a whole chapter by itself, but I will give you the basics and let your own mind and creativity fill in the gaps. When determining a business strategy you must answer six crucial questions about your business.

(1) Purpose – What is the purpose for our business? This is the most important question. It helps us answer the other five. Your business needs a purpose, what are we fulfilling in the market? Your purpose should be short, if you cannot narrow your business's purpose down to five words or less, you need to keep digging. If you can narrow it down to one word then that's even better. All your answers to the remaining five questions should be in line with your company's purpose.

(2) Who – Who are out customers? What do they want to gain and what are they trying to avoid?

(3) What – What is the best way to reach our customers using the resources we have available? And what can we do to convert them to our way of thinking? What are our price points for our product or service?

(4) When – When will we launch our business? What are our times of operation? If you are primarily marketing on Social Media, when do our followers on these platforms read, post and check-up on these platforms?

(5) Where – Where are we operating? If you have a mobile business, where will your route take you and in what order? If you have a brick and mortar business, where will its location be? If we are predominantly online, where do

we go to communicate with our potential customers and announce our business?

(6) How – How is all of this going to come together? Have we planned our budget accordingly to carry out our strategy? How is profit going to be made and how are we going to grow our business?

5) Mental Checks, Balances and Planning

Learn everything you can about the industry and how it works. Also begin to formulate a way you can work your way up the Money Chain. If you plan for it now, you won't get sidetracked later. For now just write down ideas and concept, we'll be making them official in Step Seven. Also develop your marketing. Your marketing strategy should revolve around getting your name out there using Networking, Social Media and good old pounding of the pavement. Also begin to work on your new "business role" and study all the strategies and techniques from this book you feel you may need. In other words, get your three Hustler's tools together.

6) All in the Name

Around this time, now that your vision has become clearer, you want to boil down to those few key-words that describe your business and explain its purpose. This can take some time, so be patient. It is also around this time that you should be coming up with a company name if your business will not carry your own personal name.

7) Map the Blueprint

Now that we know where we are going, we have to figure out how to get there. Look logically at how much money it's going to take to do what you need to do. Make a budget. Include the expenses for everything you can think of. Once you reach a price, double it. That will become extra cushion money in case emergencies or something costs more than you initially planned for.

The question may arise here as to whether or not you should get private investors or a bank loan. This is a question I can't answer for you. If you do go that route please do the necessary research so you don't end up in hot water later. Going this route will also require a legitimate business plan you can present to the potential investor. These can be done online now for a nominal fee or you can purchase business planning software.

If you can start on a small scale with a few hundred or thousands of dollars and are willing to build from there, then that is the route I would suggest.

It is at this time you should be designing your Up-Sell and Back-End sales strategy. How they will work and what is required to make them profitable?

As the final piece to the blueprint, you should plan now, how you are going to move up on the Money Chain. You should have a lot of ideas, now it is time narrow them down and decide on one or two. Do not forget, the higher you go, the more money there is. As your business grows we want to direct it for long term stability. Have these things in mind before day one.

8) Legalities

Now it's time for the legal stuff. Decide on your business structure. Sole proprietorship, Partnership (a dedicated partner is not an easy thing to find but can help speed things along), Limited Liability Company (LLC) or Corporation. I would suggest holding off on the corporation if you're shoe stringing, you can always get that established later once you're profitable. Just my opinion, do what's in your best interest.

Get your Employer Identification Number (EIN). This is a federal tax number and identifies your business. If you are a sole-proprietorship you will not need this because you will be filing under your social security number. This can be applied for online at the IRS website.

If you are not going to operate under your own name, you must register your trade name. A little research will let you know if this is required in your city, county and state.

Next you must get a business license. You will use your social security number or EIN for business identification. Some locations will also require a personal-property tax form. A business is taxed on 'personal' property. If it is just you and you work out of a home office, this may not be required. Or, it may not be required only for the first year in business. Anything you do acquire however needs to be recorded and reported when you file the following year.

Discover if your area requires permits. Even a home office may require a Home Occupation Permit. This determines if your home legally meets the county and/or city zoning requirements.

You also may need a seller's permit. This can also be called a certificate of resale. This allows you to collect sales tax on the products you sell. Services generally do not require this. This can be applied for online as well. Check your state website.

Remember how many businesses fail because of poor record-keeping and tax reporting? A business bank account can help in this area. Use this account for all business transactions. It should be opened under your company name and EIN.

Complete the necessary city, county and state paperwork and make sure you understand them. Also check into getting a merchant account (allows your business to take credit cards). Add this into your budget. If you need them, find a good lawyer specializing in your industry and an accountant. Again, if you're shoe stringing they may not be necessary in the beginning, but I won't advise against it. Again, your decision.

9) Building the Image

Now it's time to set up the first impression. Design and register (or trademark) your business logo (not always necessary in the early stages, but keep it in mind). Get that website up and running! If you are using a retail space (or flea market booth), now it's time to put everything in there you need along with all the services that your business will require (remember to make sure the location is correct for your business).

If it's just you in the office, don't worry about the interior appearance too much unless you plan on having clientele visit. Get business cards, flyers and/or brochures and other stationary made. If you're working exclusively online or out of a home office then make sure everything you need is there or at least accessible. A trip to *FedEx Office* every once in awhile is ok but if you live in *FedEx Office*, you need to make some adjustments as soon as possible. You need time on your side in the beginning stages.

Set up your Social Media platforms. I would recommend your Social Media platforms be under your own name and your website hold your company's name. But this really depends on your business and what you have planned for the future. Use your best judgment. There are a lot of options out there for do-it-yourself websites. I recommend weebly.com and wix.com. You can also start a blog. Blogging takes time and attention, so if that is the route you're taking make sure you can maintain it. Every Social Media platform should link to the next in some form or another.

10) Get the Word Out

Even before the Grand Opening, start networking. Meet fellow business owners, talk or find a way to get in contact with your market of future customers. The perception of you as the "expert" in your area needs to start now! Hand out those flyers and business cards. If you can, take pre-orders for your product or schedule future times to perform your service.

Under no circumstances should you forget – Do not start at a pace you cannot keep up!

11) Bring the Heat

Once you are officially open for business, celebrate but then get to work. Run your bird dog programs and market, market, market. When you're not marketing, Network. For the first few months, these two activities are the most important. More important than initial sales numbers. Remember, we want to make sure our short-term becomes bigger in the long-term.

12) Take Their Heads

This is an old Hustler saying, a little morbid I admit but we view ourselves as ancient warriors going into the battlefield with our swords drawn. We don't mean killing the competition here either (although if that helps motivate you, then by all means use that perspective – but remember it's about creation, not competition), but you're taking the heads of anything that stands in your way to your goals. Don't just take a stab at it, kill it! A nicer way to say it would be: "Kick butt and take names!"

Keep It Moving

Keep pushing, don't stop, don't get lazy or idle. You truly are your worst enemy. Always find ways to improve on what you're doing. Learn to help more people so you can see more profit. Read good books, articles, take seminars about your industry and business. Never stop learning. Translate and implement any new ideas as soon as possible in your business. As a small business you are at an advantage here. New programs and ideas are much easier to institute.

Make time to relax and spend time with your loved ones. And as you continue on your grind, don't forget to stop every once in a while and enjoy the fruits of your labor. All this work isn't for nothing.

And so we now bring this book to a close. It has been said that when the student is ready, the master will appear. I don't consider myself a master, but you have come across this information for a reason. If you accept that, "what goes around comes around," then you also have to accept this.

Don't make this just another business book. Although this has a lot of basics in it, the true power and depth of the information can only be found when you **use** it.

I have done my best to streamline and simplify everything presented here, and my sincere hope is that it motivates and inspires those who are truly looking for a way out of the "rat-race".

This isn't just another business book, it's so much more but you'll never know until you begin to use it and apply it. If some of the things in this book don't seem to apply to your business, then by all means look beneath them. Under almost every technique and principle in this book lies a law, if you will. If you can understand the truth behind a principle, you can take that and change it into something that is applicable to your business.

If this is your first time in business, then welcome to the Game! I made a strong effort to make this the book I wish I had when I started all those years ago. Again I thank you for spending this time with me and just know there is so much more to come.

About the Author

W. James Dennis started his first business when he was 17 years old. It failed. He then started his second business in his early-twenties, which failed too. But just a few years later with an example of business success to learn from, his third business did succeed and he operated it for over 10 years. During this time he was a dedicated student of the "Game", something which he calls, *Uncommon Sense*. Realizing his passion was writing and educating, he changed gears in his life and is now an author, public speaker and small business consultant living just outside of Atlanta, Georgia – United States. His favorite quote is, "Keep it moving and keep it simple in the process."

Connect with W. James Dennis

www.wjamesd.com
wjamesdennis@gmail.com
facebook.com/wjamesd
twitter: @wjamesdennis

Also by This Author

Holding Magnetic Conversations – *Learn to Be a Master Communicator in Just Hours*
Revealing the Secrets of the Game – *Exposing the Most Heavily Guarded System of Self-empowerment Ever Designed*